Series/Number 07-105

CAUSAL ANALYSIS WITH PANEL DATA

STEVEN E. FINKEL
Department of Government and Foreign Affairs
University of Virginia

SAGE PUBLICATIONS
International Educational and Professional Publisher
Thousand Oaks   London   New Delhi

For information address:

SAGE Publications, Inc.
2455 Teller Road
Thousand Oaks, California 91320

SAGE Publications Ltd.
6 Bonhill Street
London EC2A 4PU
United Kingdom

SAGE Publications India Pvt. Ltd.
M-32 Market
Greater Kailash I
New Delhi 110 048 India

Printed in the United States of America

Library of Congress Cataloging-in-Publication Data

Finkel, Steven E.
    Causal analysis with panel data / Steven E. Finkel.
        p. cm. — (Quantitative applications in the social sciences;
  vol. 105)
    Includes bibliographical references.
    ISBN 0-8039-3896-9
    1. Panel analysis. 2. Social sciences—Statistical methods.
  I. Title. II. Series: Sage university papers series. Quantitative
  applications in the social sciences; no. 105.
  H61.26.F56 1995
  300′.72—dc20   94-23667

95 96 97 98 99 10 9 8 7 6 5 4 3 2 1

Sage Project Editor: Susan McElroy

CONTENTS

SERIES EDITOR'S INTRODUCTION

Panel data are repeated over-time observations on the same sample of individual cases. A classic example is the public opinion survey, in which those sampled are interviewed twice, say in year 1 and year 2, and each time asked the same questions. A panel design has much to commend it when compared to the usual cross-sectional design. In particular, it allows stronger causal inference because it explicitly builds in the time dimension of a causal process. Consider a hypothetical illustration. Suppose a political scientist, Professor Alice Green, has been studying the relationship between left-right ideological identification (I) and vote intention (V) in a national survey (conducted at time t) of French voters. Using this cross-section, she regresses V_t on I_t (plus control variables, labeled collectively Z_t) and finds ideological identification strongly related to vote intention:

$$V_t = a + bI_t + cZ_t + e_t. \tag{I.1}$$

Professor Green suspects that that relationship is theoretically misspecified and at least partly spurious. For one, she believes that, because of "habit strength," past vote intention (V_{t-1}) influences current vote intention (V_t) and, moreover, past ideological identification (I_{t-1}) influences current ideological identification (I_t). Also, she contends that ideological identification (I_t) itself is shaped by one's vote intention (V_t). In sum, her model is as follows:

$$V_t = a + bV_{t-1} + cI_t + dZ_t + e_t. \tag{I.2}$$

$$I_t = a' + b'I_{t-1} + cV_t + c'Z_t + u_t. \tag{I.3}$$

The model captured in Equations (I.2) and (I.3) is quite different from that captured in Equation (I.1). Unfortunately, Professor Green cannot estimate this second model with the single cross-section at time t. However, if it had actually been the second wave of a panel study, with the first wave

iv

done at time $t - 1$, then she probably could (supposing, among other things, that steps were taken to assure identification of the model). This is the sort of theoretical and statistical leverage that a panel design promises.

Dr. Finkel explicates the causal inference opportunities of panel data and also shows how to overcome the analysis obstacles. In an example of the latter, he indicates the limits of ordinary least squares (OLS) regression for a model such as the one in Equations (I.2) and (I.3). Because of problems of reciprocal causation, Two Stage Least Squares or LISREL procedures, both of which he carefully describes, become necessary. Further, certain assumptions about autocorrelation may have to be met to achieve identification. In addition to these problems, measurement error can be especially serious with panel data. As he demonstrates, once it is taken into account, results can be very different. In illustrating how to cope with measurement error, he moves from the simple single-indicator, two-wave models to the more complicated, such as a three-indicator, three-wave model.

Importantly, the reader is made aware of the need to meet assumptions in order to have meaningful parameter estimates. Further, to aid the research practitioner, applications to real data are plentiful. In this respect, two data sets, one a 1987-1989 panel on West German protest behavior, the other the 1980 American National Election panel, are utilized to good effect. Dr. Finkel assumes the reader has a functional grasp of regression and LISREL and, building on this base, provides a readable but advanced treatment of panel analysis techniques.

—*Michael S. Lewis-Beck*
Series Editor

ACKNOWLEDGMENTS

I would like to thank Charles E. Denk for his invaluable advice and encouragement at various stages of this project. I am grateful to Denk, the series editor Michael Lewis-Beck, several anonymous reviewers, Karl-Dieter Opp, Timothy S. Prinz, and Janet E. Steele for their careful critiques and important suggestions for improving the manuscript. I also thank the University of Virginia's Committee on Summer Grants and Center for Advanced Studies for supporting this research during 1993-1994. Finally, the German data analyzed in the monograph were collected in collaboration with Edward N. Muller and Karl-Dieter Opp with the support of the National Science Foundation and the Stiftung Volkswagenwerk.

CAUSAL ANALYSIS WITH PANEL DATA

STEVEN E. FINKEL
Department of Government and Foreign Affairs
University of Virginia

1. INTRODUCTION

Panel data, which consist of information gathered from the same individuals or units at several different points in time, are commonly used in the social sciences to test theories of individual and social change. The most important feature of panel studies is that, in contrast to static cross-sectional analyses, change is explicitly incorporated into the design so that individual (or other unit-level) changes in a set of variables are directly measured. Panel data may also be distinguished from two other forms of longitudinal data (Menard, 1991): "repeated cross-section" or "trend" data, which consist of information collected on the same variables for *different* units over time; and "time series" data, which consist of observations collected on several variables for a *single* unit at multiple points in time (Ostrom, 1978). The distinctiveness of panel data is that they contain measures of the same variables from numerous units observed repeatedly through time.[1]

This monograph provides an overview of models appropriate for the analysis of panel data, focusing specifically on the area where panels offer major advantages over cross-sectional research designs: the analysis of causal interrelationships among variables. For a causal effect to exist from variable X to variable Y, the following well-known conditions must be met (Menard, 1991, p. 17): (a) X and Y must covary, as evidenced in nonexperimental studies by a nonzero bivariate correlation; (b) X must precede Y in time; and (c) the relationship must not be "spurious," or produced by X and Y's joint association with a third variable or set of variables. Successful causal inference also depends on the accurate measurement of the variables of interest because statistical estimation of causal effects will yield incorrect results when random or nonrandom measurement errors in observed variables are not taken into account (Berry & Feldman, 1985; Carmines &

1

Zeller, 1979). Cross-sectional data can provide evidence regarding the first condition of covariation, but their usefulness in providing evidence regarding time precedence and nonspuriousness, and in specifying models that correct for measurement error in the variables, is much more limited. As will become evident, panel data offer decided advantages in all of these areas.

In cross-sectional analyses, the measurement of variables at a single time point makes it difficult to establish temporal order, and hence to rule out the possibility that covariation between X and Y is produced by Y causing X, or through a reciprocal causal relationship. By contrast, the observation of X and Y through time on the same units in panel analyses enables the researcher to specify certain models that necessarily satisfy the time precedence criterion, that is, where prior values of each variable may affect later values of the other. Further, in instances where reciprocal causality is suspected, the panel analyst may estimate nonrecursive models with feedback effects between variables with fewer restrictive assumptions than in the cross-sectional case. Panel data are also useful in controlling for the effects of outside variables that may render the relationship between X and Y either partially or fully spurious. Whereas spurious association in cross-sectional analysis can be tested only by actually including the outside variables in the statistical model, in panel studies certain patterns of spuriousness caused by *unmeasured* factors may also be tested against the data. Finally, measurement error models can be estimated with panel data with fewer restrictive assumptions than are necessary in the cross-sectional context, as the analyst can utilize the additional observations over time to estimate both causal effects and measurement properties of the variables. In all of these ways, panel designs allow more rigorous tests of causal relations than are possible with cross-sections, and thus approximate more closely than other observational research designs the controlled testing of causality possible with experimental methods.

Throughout the monograph, two complementary perspectives on causal analysis with panel data will be presented. It will be shown that panel data offer multiple ways of strengthening the causal inference process, and succeeding chapters will demonstrate how to estimate models that contain a variety of lag specifications, reciprocal effects, and imperfectly measured variables. At the same time, it will be emphasized that panel data are not a cure-all for the problems of causal inference in nonexperimental research. All of the procedures and models that will be presented depend on their own set of assumptions that must be justified in a given situation. If these assumptions are untenable or yield implausible empirical results, alternative models must be estimated and compared before the researcher can have confidence in the causal conclusions drawn from the analyses.

Since the publication of Markus's earlier monograph in this series, *Analyzing Panel Data* (1979), the literature on panel analysis has grown tremendously. This monograph attempts to highlight the contributions made by scholars from diverse disciplines and analytic traditions. Certain topics, however, could not be covered adequately in a single work. The monograph concentrates, for example, on linear models for the analysis of interval-level dependent variables; Markus (1979, Chapter 2) provides an introduction to techniques for the analysis of discrete panel data and Plewis (1985, Chapters 6-7) summarizes more recent work. The discussion here is also limited to issues of estimation and interpretation of panel models, ignoring issues related to panel attrition and mortality and biases related to self-selection of panel respondents. Readers are referred to Kessler and Greenberg (1981, Chapter 12) and Menard (1991, Chapter 4) for excellent treatments of these topics.

Readers will profit most from the presentation that follows if they are already familiar with multiple regression analysis and causal modeling methods at least to the level of the previous monographs in this series (Asher, 1983; Berry, 1984; Berry & Feldman, 1985). It is also recommended that readers become familiar with more general structural equation methods such as LISREL or EQS, as these procedures are now routine tools for panel analysis. See Long (1983a, 1983b) for an introduction to LISREL; more detailed discussions of LISREL and alternative methods can be found in Bollen (1989), Bentler (1985), Hayduk (1987), Jöreskog and Sörbom (1976), McArdle and Aber (1990), and McDonald (1980). At some points in the monograph, models will be presented and discussed using the LISREL framework to facilitate the application of these procedures, but the models also may be estimated with EQS and other structural equation packages. The Appendix contains an overview of the LISREL notational structure.

2. MODELING CHANGE WITH PANEL DATA

Panel data contain measures of variables for each individual or unit at time t and at other time points $t-1$, $t-2$, and so on, depending on the number of waves of observations. Hence it is possible to use information about *prior* as well as current values of variables in constructing and estimating causal models. The presence of lagged Y, or the "lagged endogenous" variable, allows us to analyze explicitly the *changes* in Y over time, and if we can show that a variable X is associated with changes in Y (ΔY), this would represent more direct evidence of a causal effect from X to Y than is possible to obtain in static cross-sectional designs. Moreover, the presence of both lagged and current values of X in a panel data set allows a variety of alternative specifications of the causal effect of X on Y. In addition to estimating the effect of X_{t-1} on ΔY, the researcher may construct a variable representing the change in X between panel waves and model Y or ΔY as a function of X_{t-1}, X_t, ΔX, or some combination of these variables.

However, although the presence of current and lagged values of X and Y gives the researcher critical additional information with which to analyze change, the proper method of specifying the effects of these variables in panel models is not obvious. In this chapter, we will show that, in most cases, the preferred model for panel analysis will be some variant of a "static-score" or "conditional change" equation predicting the current value of the dependent variable Y_t with its lagged value Y_{t-1} and a series of X independent variables. We then show that the choice of X_t, X_{t-1}, and/or ΔX as independent variables will depend on the length of time between panel observations and on different theoretical assumptions about the nature and timing of the causal lag from X to Y. Finally, in subsequent chapters we address in more detail several potential problems in the estimation and interpretation of panel models.

Change-Score Models and the Role of Lagged Endogenous Variables

The "Unconditional" Change-Score Model

One possible method for estimating the effects of an independent variable X on change in a dependent variable Y with panel data begins with an extension of the model usually found in cross-sectional analyses:

$$Y_t = \beta_0 + \beta_1 X_t + \epsilon_t \tag{2.1}$$

where Y_t and X_t are the values for the dependent and independent variables for an individual or case at time t, and ϵ_t is the error term. The equation can be extended with no additional complications to include other observed independent variables, but we present the simple two-variable model here for ease of exposition. With panel data, the same variables are measured at more than one point in time, and the additional waves of measurement can be used to provide important information with which to estimate the model's parameters. Assuming that the independent variable changes to some extent in the interval between measurements, and that the same causal process between X and Y holds at time $t - 1$, that is, $\beta_{1t-1} = \beta_{1t}$, then subtracting from (2.1) a similar equation using values of X, Y, and ϵ at time $t - 1$ yields the following:

$$Y_t - Y_{t-1} = (\beta_{0t} - \beta_{0t-1}) + \beta_1 (X_t - X_{t-1}) + (\epsilon_t - \epsilon_{t-1})$$

or   (2.2)

$$\Delta Y = \Delta \beta_0 + \beta_1 \Delta X + \Delta \epsilon .$$

This equation represents the simple regression of the change in Y on the change in X, and is thus referred to as the *"unconditional" change-score* approach to panel analysis, or the *method of first differences* (Allison, 1990; Liker, Augustyniak, & Duncan, 1985).

This equation is superior to its cross-sectional counterpart (2.1) in several ways. First, by using the actual change scores in the analysis, it models the determinants of individual- or unit-level changes in variables directly, as opposed to cross-sectional analyses in which regression estimates of the "changes" in an independent variable on "changes" in a dependent variable are based solely on interunit variations at one point in time. This advantage is common to all panel models. More specifically, the unconditional change-score approach provides a control for certain kinds of omitted explanatory variables in (2.1), or what are referred to in the econometric literature as *individual permanent effects*. If the true explanatory model includes some *unchanging* independent variables (Z) that are either unknown or for some reason cannot be included in the model, as in

$$Y_t = \beta_0 + \beta_1 X_t + \beta_2 Z + \epsilon_t ,$$ (2.3)

then the cross-sectional estimates of β_1 will be biased to the extent that X and the Zs are correlated (because the Zs are effectively lumped into the error term of Equation [2.1]).

However, if the effects of the omitted Z variables on Y are assumed to be constant over time, then they drop out of Equation (2.2) completely through the differencing process:

$$\Delta Y = \Delta \beta_0 + \beta_1 \Delta X + \beta_2 \Delta Z + \Delta \epsilon$$

$$\Delta Y = \Delta \beta_0 + \beta_1 \Delta X + \Delta \epsilon .$$

(2.4)

Because the confounding influences of Z have been removed in (2.4), the independent variable ΔX is no longer correlated with the error term $\Delta \epsilon$, as X_t and X_{t-1} from Equation (2.3) are assumed to be uncorrelated with ϵ_t and ϵ_{t-1}, respectively. Hence Equation (2.4) yields unbiased estimates of the causal effect of X on Y, and the difference between the estimate of β_1 from Equations (2.1) and (2.4) indicates the degree of misspecification bias in the cross-sectional model (2.1) because of the omission of relevant stable Z variables. Thus with this specification, "panel data allow for the consistent estimation of the effects of the independent variables in the model even though the model is only partially specified" (Arminger, 1987, p. 339), a clear advantage of panels compared to cross-sectional models.

However, although the first difference or unconditional change-score panel model can be useful in estimating parameters in these types of misspecified models, it contains one highly restrictive assumption: that the lagged dependent (or "lagged endogenous") variable Y_{t-1} does not have an influence on either Y_t or ΔY. As we will see, this assumption is likely to be incorrect, and for this reason the unconditional change model usually fails as a structural model for analyzing change.[2]

The Static-Score or Conditional Change Model

Including the lagged dependent variable in Equation (2.1) yields what is referred to as the *static-score* or *conditional change* panel model (Plewis, 1985):

$$Y_t = \beta_0 + \beta_1 X_t + \beta_2 Y_{t-1} + \epsilon_t .$$

(2.5)

In this model, Y_t is predicted from its earlier value Y_{t-1}, from the independent variable X at the same time period, and from a random error term assumed (for now) to have constant variance, no autocorrelation, and no correlation with either X_t or Y_{t-1}. When X is not constant and has been measured at several points in time, the effects of X_{t-1} and possibly other lag values of X may also be included in the model, as will be discussed below.

This model may also be expressed in terms of ΔY, the change in the dependent variable over time, by simply subtracting Y_{t-1} from Equation (2.5) to yield

$$\Delta Y = \beta_0 + \beta_1 X_t + (\beta_2 - 1) Y_{t-1} + \epsilon_t . \qquad (2.6)$$

From this specification, it can be seen that β_1, the causal effect of X on Y in the static-score model, can also be interpreted as the causal effect of X on ΔY, controlling for initial values of the dependent variable, and the effect of Y_{t-1} on ΔY in Equation (2.6) is simply the "stability" effect of Y_{t-1} on Y_t in Equation (2.5) minus 1.

The unconditional change model discussed previously may also be expressed in terms of Y_t and Y_{t-1} by moving Y_{t-1} to the right-hand side of Equation (2.4) and constraining its causal effect to equal 1:

$$Y_t = \Delta\beta_0 + \beta_1 \Delta X + Y_{t-1} + \Delta\epsilon . \qquad (2.7)$$

It is sometimes argued that the unconditional change model is only a constrained version of the static-score formulation (Hendrickson & Jones, 1987). This is incorrect insofar as Y_{t-1} is *necessarily* correlated with $(\epsilon_t - \epsilon_{t-1})$, the error term in Equation (2.7), whereas Y_{t-1} is assumed to be uncorrelated with ϵ_t, the error term in Equation (2.5) (Allison, 1990, p. 103). This means that the two models are fundamentally different in their specifications, and the decision for the analyst is whether to estimate the unconditional change model of Equation (2.4) or the static-score model (2.5) or (2.6). There are several arguments that support the choice in most nonexperimental studies of the static-score model.

Substantive Justifications of the Static-Score Model

First, there may be substantive reasons for assuming that Y_{t-1} is a cause of either Y_t or ΔY. In the analyses of political, social, or psychological attitudes, prior orientations may exert some causal effect on either current outlooks or changes in orientations over time. Individuals who, for example, approve of the sitting President's performance in one month may be likely to approve of his performance again next month at least partially because of their prior attitudes. As another example, it is likely that an individual's prior income is not simply a good predictor of current income, but rather may have some causal effect on current income, as wealthy individuals may have investment strategies that will tend to increase their earnings to a greater extent than will economic decisions made by the poor (Plewis, 1985, p. 59). In bureaucratic decision-making models, it is often assumed that an agency's budget or expenditures in past years exerts some causal influence on the present year's value. In general, whenever the present state of the dependent variable (or change in the dependent variable) is determined directly from past states, inclusion of the lagged dependent variable in these situations is necessary to specify the model properly. On the other hand, when variables need to be "created anew" in each time period, there will be no substantive basis for including prior values as predictors of current states.[3]

Regression to the Mean

Even when there is no clear substantive reason for the inclusion of lagged Y, the static-score model often can be justified on statistical grounds. The reason is that omitting lagged Y does not take into account one of the most pervasive phenomena in the analysis of change: the likely *negative* correlation between initial scores on a variable and subsequent change, or what is known more generally as "regression to the mean." By ignoring the tendency of individuals or units with large values on Y at one point in time to have smaller values at a subsequent time, and the tendency of individuals with small values on Y to have larger subsequent values, the unconditional change-score model leads to biased results to the extent that explanatory variables X (or ΔX) are related to the initial values of Y.

"Regression effects" leading to a negative correlation between Y_{t-1} and ΔY occur in panel data for a variety of reasons. One reason is the presence of random measurement error in Y, because one source of large values on Y_{t-1} could be large errors of measurement, which would tend to be smaller in the next wave. In the extreme case in which there was no "true" change in Y at all, *all* observed change would be due to measurement error, and it can be shown that the covariance between Y_{t-1} and ΔY would equal the negative of the error variance in Y whenever the measurement error variances were equal over time (Dwyer, 1983, p. 339). But "regression to the mean" also can exist in panel models with perfect measurement. Because extreme scores on Y_{t-1} are caused in part by large error terms ϵ_{t-1}, representing the effects of all omitted variables as well as purely random factors, change in Y likely will be negatively related to Y_{t-1}, as the error terms will tend to be smaller in the next wave of measurement. If this is the case, then omitting Y_{t-1} will lead to a downward bias in the estimated effect on ΔY of any independent variable X that is positively related to both Y_t and Y_{t-1}.

Regression effects are not always present in panel data, but it can be shown that a negative correlation between a variable's initial value and subsequent change can be expected whenever (a) the variable is not perfectly correlated over time and (b) its variance is relatively constant (Bohrnstedt, 1969; Kessler & Greenberg, 1981; Nesselroade, Stigler, & Baltes, 1980). Under these circumstances, including Y_{t-1} in the regression model is a way of controlling for this phenomenon, and frames the analysis in the following fashion: Do the independent X variables influence changes in Y for fixed levels of Y_{t-1}, that is, taking into account the negative effect of initial values of Y on subsequent change? As will be shown in Chapter 4, however, further corrections will be necessary if regression effects are caused by measurement errors in Y_{t-1}.

Negative Feedback

Another justification for the inclusion of lagged Y in panel models stems from the concept of the *stability* of social systems. A causal system is said to be "stable" if it will approach at some future time period a fixed equilibrium point where the values of Y for each case will be constant until the system is altered by some exogenous disturbance (Arminger, 1987; Dwyer, 1983). Given that most systems analyzed in empirical research have not yet reached equilibrium, it can be shown that system stability *requires* a "negative feedback" effect from Y_{t-1} to ΔY (Coleman, 1968). If the effect of Y_{t-1} on ΔY is positive, then Y will expand without limit: If Y_{t-1} is negative, then Y will become more and more negative over time, whereas if Y_{t-1} is positive, then Y will become more and more positive. In either case, the variance of Y will "explode," a situation that is considered unlikely (although not technically impossible) in most social-psychological systems. Hence the negative effect from Y_{t-1} on ΔY steers the system toward equilibrium; when Y is above its equilibrium level, it will decline, and when Y is below its equilibrium level, it will increase.

Such negative feedback of Y_{t-1} on ΔY also has been interpreted as a proxy for causal paths linking Y_{t-1} to Y_t through variables that are omitted from the model. Coleman (1968) asserts that the positive effect of Y_{t-1} on Y_t (and hence the negative effect of Y_{t-1} on ΔY) can be viewed

as a surrogate for all the chains of feedback in the empirical system that remain implicit in the formal system. As the formal system becomes more complete, this coefficient should approach zero. Thus the size of the coefficient allows a way of evaluating the completeness of any representation of the empirical system. (p. 441)

In this view, taking into account the prior level of the dependent variable serves to control at least partially for omitted variables that influence the changes in Y_t. In this role, however, lagged Y has a different "epistemelogical status" than as a variable that exerts direct causal influence on Y_t in a substantive sense, and its estimated effect should be interpreted accordingly (Arminger, 1987; Liker et al., 1985).

Partial Adjustment

Finally, lagged Y may be included in some panel models in order to estimate other theoretically relevant parameters of interest. One example is the *partial adjustment* model first popularized in economics. In this model, some unknown "desired," "optimal," or "target" value (Y_t^*), rather than the actual value of the dependent variable (Y_t), is assumed to be accounted for by the explanatory variables, so that the underlying substantive equation would be

$$Y_t^* = \beta_0 + \beta_1 X_t + \epsilon_t. \tag{2.8}$$

Y_t^* is often viewed as the equilibrium level of Y as described above, but the desired value Y^* may also represent other targets, such as the objective of an organization or, in rational action terms, the value of Y that gives the individual maximum utility (Tuma & Hannan, 1984, p. 339).

According to this model, individuals or organizations strive to minimize the difference between Y^* and Y over time, but the *actual* change in Y would equal only some fraction α of the difference between Y_t^* and Y_{t-1}. That is, because of inertia, ignorance, or structural factors impeding change, there would be in each time period only a "partial adjustment" of the gap between the desired and actual values of Y. This idea may be expressed as

$$Y_t - Y_{t-1} = \alpha(Y_t^* - Y_{t-1}) \tag{2.9}$$

where the coefficient α represents the adjustment coefficient, or the extent to which the gap between the desired and actual values are narrowed from time $t - 1$ to time t. Substituting the value of Y_t^* from Equation (2.8) into Equation (2.9) yields the estimation equation

$$Y_t - Y_{t-1} = \alpha\beta_0 + -\alpha Y_{t-1} + \alpha\beta_1 X_t + \alpha\epsilon_t, \tag{2.10}$$

which has the same general form as the conditional change model (2.6), with ΔY being predicted from Y_{t-1} and X_t. It can be seen from Equation (2.10) that the regression effect of Y_{t-1} on ΔY will equal the negative of the adjustment parameter α; the closer the estimated effect is to -1, the more Y adjusts to its "desired" or equilibrium value in a given time period. The regression effect for X_t obtained from estimating Equation (2.10) can be interpreted in two ways: In its raw form, it represents the short-term effect of X_t on Y or ΔY across the panel waves; dividing this value by α gives the value of β_1 in Equation (2.8), which represents the long-run effect of X_t on the equilibrium or desired value Y_t^*. The partial adjustment model thus provides a different, although complementary, justification for the inclusion of Y_{t-1} as a predictor of ΔY in panel models.[4]

Estimation of the Static-Score Model

We illustrate the static-score model with data from a 1987-1989 panel survey of West Germans ($N = 377$) that was undertaken to model individual participation in political protest activities (see Finkel, Muller, & Opp, 1989, for more details on the study and sampling procedures). The variables of interest here, measured in both waves, are individual scores on a logged *legal protest potential* index (PROTEST$_1$ and PROTEST$_2$), measured through a combination of future behavioral intentions weighted by past participation in eight nonviolent behaviors, such as collecting signatures for a petition and participating in a legal demonstration, and a *group memberships* index (GROUPS$_1$ and GROUPS$_2$) that represents the number of groups to which respondents belong that they claim encourage protest behavior. Protest potential at time $t - 1$ may be linked to protest potential at time t through a partial adjustment process, whereby Y_t^* would represent the level of protest that would maximize individual utility, and the group memberships variable (GROUPS$_2$) would represent one component of the social pressure or group mobilization processes by which individuals would derive utility from participation. For this reason, as well as for the statistical reasons described above, we specify the static-score panel model to represent the relationship between X and Y over time. We assume in this chapter that the causal relationship between GROUPS and PROTEST is unidirectional.

If it is assumed that the error term in the static-score model is uncorrelated with both X_t and Y_{t-1}, then the coefficients can be estimated *consistently* through ordinary least squares (OLS) regression. OLS normally produces estimates, given these assumptions, that are both consistent (i.e., approach the true population value as N goes to infinity) and unbiased (i.e., neither overestimate nor underestimate the true parameter in an infinite number of estimates from random samples), but when lagged dependent variables are included in recursive models, OLS estimates contain a bias that is reduced to zero as N becomes larger and larger (Johnston, 1972). Hence OLS estimates in the presence of lagged dependent variables are consistent, although not technically unbiased. The results from the OLS estimation are

$$\text{PROTEST}_2 = \underset{(.02)}{.22} + \underset{\underset{\underline{.30}}{(.02)}}{.10}\ \text{GROUPS}_2 + \underset{\underset{\underline{.40}}{(.04)}}{.40}\ \text{PROTEST}_1 \qquad (2.11)$$

with standard errors in parentheses, standardized coefficients underscored, and a model R^2 of .34. The results indicate that, controlling for initial levels of the dependent variable, each additional group to which the individual belongs in 1989 increases the logged protest potential scale in 1989 by .10, and this effect is statistically significant at conventional levels. The model also can be interpreted to mean that each additional membership group in 1989 leads to a .10 *change* in legal protest potential between 1987 and 1989, controlling for initial levels of protest. The stability effect of protest in 1987 on protest in 1989 is .40, and this effect is also statistically significant; an equivalent interpretation is that protest in 1987 has a $(.40 - 1)$, or $-.60$, effect on the *change* in protest between the two waves. From the partial adjustment perspective, we calculate α as .60, indicating that protest adjusts by 60% to its optimal (equilibrium) level from one time period to the next. The long-run causal effects of each increase in the group memberships index on the optimal or equilibrium level of protest potential is .17 (.10 divided by .60 or, following Equation [2.10], the estimated β_1 divided by α).

Alternative Lag Specifications

The model just estimated stipulates that the independent variable GROUPS has an effect on PROTEST at the same point in time, that is, X_t is presumed to cause Y_t. Actually it cannot be claimed that X causes Y "instantaneously," but rather that the causal lag for X to influence Y is short, relative to the time elapsed between waves of measurement.[5] But this specification of a "synchronous" or "cotemporal" effect is only one of several that can be exploited with panel data in order to determine the causal effect of X on Y. If the time lag necessary for X to influence Y is sufficiently long but still shorter than the time between panel waves, then a lagged effects model will be more appropriate, where Y_t is a function of Y_{t-1} and X_{t-1}. If X is highly stable over time, then the choice of specifications makes little difference because estimating a causal effect from either X_{t-1} or X_t on Y_t will produce similar results. But if X changes significantly between waves of measurement, then the possible bias from misspecification of the causal lag is considerable.

The problem of specifying the appropriate lag structure for the effects of variables on one another is one of the most difficult issues in panel (and other longitudinal) analyses, and occurs for two general reasons. First, the researcher is often uncertain about the length of time it should take theoretically for X to exert its effect on Y. If a person joins a protest-oriented group or secondary organization, will it take 1 day, 1 week, 3 months, or 6 months for his or her own protest inclinations to intensify? Second, even if the theoretical causal lag were known, there is no guarantee that this time period would correspond to the time period between waves of observation because administrative convenience, funding availability, and the like determine the measurement period in panel studies at least as often as do substantive concerns. Given this uncertainty, the specification of lag structures in panel analysis should be guided first by theoretical concerns and second by empirical evidence in a given research situation.

Discrete Time Panel Models

One important aspect of the lag relationship between X and Y is whether change is assumed to occur in discrete "jumps" or continuously through time. For example, changes in congressional election outcomes occur in a fixed interval of 2 years, whereas changes in evaluations of the President can occur more or less continuously throughout a 4-year term in office. Panel models for continuous time processes have been developed by Coleman (1968) and more recently by Tuma and Hannan (1984), and we describe these methods in more detail in the next section. If change is assumed to occur in discrete time, then the lag structure should be specified on the basis of a priori expectations about how long it should take X to influence Y, coupled with knowledge of the time period between waves of measurement of the panel. When there is no clear theoretical guidance regarding the appropriate lag length for model specification, then the analyst may attempt to determine the causal lag empirically.

For example, we will analyze in later chapters the effect of an adolescent's involvement with a delinquent peer group on his or her own delinquent behavior. In this case, a relatively short causal lag between X and Y may be expected, as it would be unreasonable to expect an adolescent's peer group 2 or 3 years in the past to influence current behavior. Consequently, if panel data were gathered at 3-year intervals, a "lagged effect" model would not be the appropriate specification, and an "instantaneous" effect model might better capture the causal effect of delinquent peers on youth delinquency. However, if the data were gathered at 1- or 2-month intervals, this might coincide better with the actual time it would take for the social pressure, planning, and so on in a peer group to result in delinquent behavior, and a lagged specification would be appropriate.

Theoretical concerns might also dictate that a model include both lagged and instantaneous effects. Consider the effect of stressful or traumatic life events on an individual's psychological well-being. Given panel observations of 1 or 2 years, it may be expected that stressful life events influence psychological health in the current period. At the same time, stressful events from 2 years previous to the current observation (X_{t-1}) may also have some lingering direct effects on current psychological health, or have indirect influence on current well-being through unmeasured variables such as the individual's physical condition, job performance, and the like (Kessler & Greenberg, 1981, pp. 78-79).

With unidirectional causal models, the inclusion of both X_t and X_{t-1} in the model poses no serious problems for estimation (aside from the possibility of high multicollinearity when the variable is extremely stable), and so a model of the following form can be estimated that may shed some light on the appropriate lag relationship:

$$Y_t = \beta_0 + \beta_1 X_t + \beta_2 Y_{t-1} + \beta_3 X_{t-1} + \epsilon_t. \tag{2.12}$$

Such a formulation may also be a more intuitively appealing representation of the relationship between changes in both the independent and the dependent variables over time. The coefficients of this equation also can be recast in terms of the changes in X by making use of the identity $X_t = X_{t-1} + \Delta X$. Thus Equation (2.12) can be expressed as

$$Y_t = \beta_0 + \beta_2 Y_{t-1} + (\beta_1 + \beta_3) X_{t-1} + \beta_1 \Delta X + \epsilon_t. \tag{2.13}$$

Note that β_1, the effect of ΔX on Y_t in Equation (2.13), is the same as the effect of X_t on Y_t in (2.12); in other words, saying that the *change* in X has some effect on Y_t means that X_t has some effect on Y_t, controlling for X and Y's prior values (Kessler & Greenberg, 1981, p. 10).

The parameters of Equation (2.13) can be obtained through these algebraic manipulations or obtained directly (including their associated standard errors) by including X_1 and ΔX as explanatory variables in a regression model. Similar manipulations can be performed to transform Equation (2.12) into expressions for ΔX and X_2 as well.[6] Because the models are algebraically equivalent, the substantive interpretation of the results will depend on the theoretical assumptions of the model. In models of political stability, for example, it may be plausible to assume that instability is linked negatively to a country's current economic level (X_2) but affected positively by changes in economic level over some period of time (ΔX), as the hypothesis of rapid economic growth as a "destabilizing force" suggests. Models of political campaign effects on voters might assume that an individual's vote depended on some initial characteristics such as approval of the incumbent administration's performance (X_1) as well as changes in approval (ΔX) that were induced by events or otherwise took place during the campaign (Finkel, 1993). Thus equations that include current and lagged values of X as predictors of the changes in Y can be interpreted in a variety of ways depending on the substantive concerns of the model.

We reestimate the static-score model from the group memberships-protest example by including GROUPS$_1$, the group memberships variable from 1987, as a predictor of protest potential in 1989. Theoretically, the effect of group memberships on protest may be lagged to some degree if protest behaviors organized by groups are planned far enough in advance. On the other hand, the 2-year time difference between panel observations may represent too long a lag length, in which case the synchronous effects model would be superior. The OLS estimates support this contention. The pure lagged effects model, with Y_t predicted from X_{t-1} and Y_{t-1}, shows a much weaker effect from GROUPS to PROTEST than in the synchronous model of Equation (2.13):

$$\text{PROTEST}_2 = \underset{(.02)}{.22} + \underset{\underset{.11}{(.02)}}{.04 \text{ GROUPS}_1} + \underset{\underset{.47}{(.05)}}{.47 \text{ PROTEST}_1} \quad (2.14)$$

with standard errors in parentheses, standardized coefficients underscored, and an R^2 of .28, which is weaker than in the synchronous model. Estimating a static-score model with both GROUPS$_1$ and GROUPS$_2$ as independent variables yields the following results:

$$PROTEST_2 = \qquad\qquad\qquad\qquad\qquad\qquad\qquad (2.15)$$

$$.22 \;+\; .11\,GROUPS_2 \;+\; -.01\,GROUPS_1 \;+\; .40\,PROTEST_1$$
$$(.02) \qquad (.02) \qquad\qquad (-.02) \qquad\qquad (.04)$$
$$\underline{.31} \qquad\qquad \underline{-.02} \qquad\qquad \underline{.40}$$

with standard errors in parentheses, standardized coefficients underscored, and an R^2 value of .34. The results indicate that current group memberships is significantly related to protest potential, controlling for lagged Y and lagged group memberships. Controlling for current group memberships, lagged group memberships is statistically insignificant and adds little additional explanatory power to the model. Following Equation (2.13), the effect of GROUPS$_2$ also may be interpreted as the effect of the *changes* in group memberships on PROTEST$_2$, controlling for lagged group memberships and lagged protest potential.

Panel Models in Continuous Time

The previous section discussed procedures for estimating the proper lag structure for the effects of X to be felt on Y over a given time interval. If the theoretical lag length matched the length of time between waves of observation, a lagged effects model would be preferred, whereas if the lag length was much shorter than the length between waves, a synchronous effects model would be superior. In some panel models, however, the influence of X on Y can be viewed as occurring more or less *continuously* through time, rather than in a discrete jump between the waves of observation of the panel. For example, the effect of individuals' party affiliations on their attitudes about presidential candidates might operate continuously throughout a campaign, as individuals may constantly adjust their ratings of the major party candidates in response to their underlying party loyalties as time progressed. Organizations might adjust their employment base more or less continuously in response to economic forces in the environment. Such models have much intuitive and theoretical appeal for analyzing many of the dependent variables typically studied by social scientists, such as attitudes and other social-psychological constructs, organizational change, and population movements. In these cases, measurements taken at particular times in a given panel study represent purely arbitrary time intervals for the observations of the causal process to have been made, and the task of the analyst is to uncover what Coleman (1968) calls the "fundamental parameters of change." As will be seen, the methods involved in estimating continuous and discrete time models are similar, but the interpretation of the parameters differs significantly.

We express the basic continuous time model by modeling the derivative of Y with respect to time t as

$$\frac{dY_t}{dt} = c_0 + c_1 X_t + c_2 Y_t. \tag{2.16}$$

The derivative of Y with respect to t is the term from elementary calculus that represents the instantaneous rate of change in Y, that is, the amount of change in Y as t changes by an infinitesimal amount. According to this equation, this quantity is determined by both X and Y at a given point in time. Many other models predicting the rate of change in Y are possible, for example, a prediction of the rate of change as a constant value or as a function of time itself, but the formulation in Equation (2.16) is of most theoretical interest, as it models the instantaneous rate of change in Y as a function of Y and variables that are also hypothesized to have causal effects on Y_t.

In order to estimate the model, the differential equation is solved, or "integrated," which results in an expression for current Y in terms of the cumulative effects of variables in Equation (2.16) over the interval from $t - 1$ to t. Assuming for now that the exogenous variable X is constant over time, integrating Equation (2.16) leads to the following solution:

$$Y_t = \frac{c_0}{c_2}(e^{c_2 \Delta t} - 1) + \frac{c_1}{c_2}(e^{c_2 \Delta t} - 1)X + e^{c_2 \Delta t}Y_{t-1} \tag{2.17}$$

where e is the natural logarithm and Δt is the time between panel waves. If a random error term is added to Equation (2.17) to summarize other causes of Y_t, it can be seen that the equation is another version of the static-score model (2.5), with X and Y_{t-1} as independent variables predicting Y_t:

$$Y_t = \beta_0 + \beta_1 X + \beta_2 Y_{t-1} + \epsilon_t. \tag{2.18}$$

Unlike the regression coefficients in the discrete time case, however, the β_k in the continuous time estimation model represent complex nonlinear functions of the c coefficients in Equation (2.17) and of the time period

18

between waves of measurement. But given the standard assumptions regarding the error term, as well as the assumption of no specification or measurement errors, the β_k can be estimated with OLS, and the c coefficients above, corresponding to the "fundamental parameters of change," can be recovered as

$$c_0 = \beta_0 \frac{\ln \beta_2}{\Delta t (\beta_2 - 1)}$$

$$c_1 = \beta_1 \frac{\ln \beta_2}{\Delta t (\beta_2 - 1)} \tag{2.19}$$

$$c_2 = \frac{\ln \beta_2}{\Delta t}.$$

An Example

This procedure is illustrated with data from the 1980 American National Election panel study, which contains interviews with a random sample of 763 voting-age adults in January, June, September, and November, 1980. Research on attitude change during presidential campaigns suggests that opinions about candidates depend directly on individuals' party loyalties, so that individuals who are strongly committed to the Republican or Democratic party are likely to rate their own party's candidate more *positively* at the end of a campaign than at the beginning, whereas they will rate the candidate of the opposing party more *negatively* over time (Markus, 1982). In this study, individuals were asked to rate the two major party candidates, Republican Ronald Reagan and Democrat Jimmy Carter, on 100-point "feeling thermometer" scales, and a variable representing the differences in ratings of the two candidates was constructed so that positive scores indicate a relatively warmer rating for Reagan and negative scores indicate a relatively warmer rating for Carter. We call the June variable $THERM_1$ and the September variable $THERM_2$ in the analyses that follow. Using a 7-point party identification scale in June (PID_1), running from "strong Democrat" to "strong Republican," as the independent variable, the following coefficients, standard errors, and standardized results are obtained from OLS estimation of Equation (2.18):

$$\text{THERM}_2 = \underset{(.99)}{-2.05} + \underset{\underset{.20}{(.54)}}{3.74\ \text{PID}_1} + \underset{\underset{.65}{(.03)}}{.66\ \text{THERM}_1} \qquad (2.20)$$

Both independent variables' coefficients are statistically significant, and the overall R^2 for this model is .59. The estimates provide support for the hypothesis of partisan polarization in thermometer ratings over the course of the 1980 campaign. Each unit pro-Republican increase in party identification is associated with a statistically significant 3.74 unit pro-Reagan (or anti-Carter) change in the individual's relative feeling thermometer ratings of the candidates between June and September. The effect of June thermometer ratings on September levels, controlling for party identification, is .66; equivalently, the model indicates that the effect of June ratings on the *change* in thermometer scores between June and September is −.34 (.66 − 1).

From the continuous time perspective, the coefficients in Equation (2.20) are used to solve for the c coefficients in the underlying differential equation that summarizes the effect of party identification on the instantaneous rate of change in candidate evaluations over time. According to the equalities shown in Equation (2.19), the effect of candidate ratings (Y_{t-1}) on the derivative of Y with respect to t is −.14, and the effect of party identification (X_{t-1}) is 1.53, assuming a value of 3 for Δt to correspond to the 3-month time interval between panel measurements. The estimated constant, c_0, is .88.

These coefficients yield important information about the nature of this causal system. First, the system is stable, that is, it eventually will equilibrate because of the "negative feedback" effect represented by the −.14 c_2 coefficient. Second, the equilibrium value of Y for a given case can be calculated by setting the differential equation to zero and solving for Y as $(-c_0 - c_1 X_1)/c_2$. Thus, if an individual's party identification at the beginning of the campaign is at 3, corresponding to a strong Republican, the model predicts the equilibrium value of Y to be 39.1 on the thermometer differential scale, whereas the equilibrium value for a strong Democrat (with a party identification score of −3) is −26.5. Third, the size of the c_2 coefficient indicates the speed at which Y moves toward its equilibrium value. If c_2 is very small (i.e., with very large negative values) then Y moves toward equilibrium very quickly as a result of the exogenous effect from X. As c_2 becomes larger, Y approaches the steady state slowly through time. In this case, the value of −.14 for c_2 indicates a relatively slow path toward equilibrium. If the underlying substantive model is conceived as a partial adjustment process whereby Y adjusts toward some target or expected utility goal then it can be shown that the adjustment parameter α is equal to the negative of the c_2 coefficient in Equation (2.16) (Tuma & Hannan, 1984, pp. 337-338). In this case, the estimated α is .14, indicating, as in the equilibrium interpretation, that Y adjusts very slowly to the desired target.

The continuous time model can be extended to handle situations in which exogenous variables change throughout the period of the panel observations. In order to recover the c coefficients from the differential Equation (2.16) in this case, some assumptions must be made regarding how X changes over time. Given a simple assumption that X changes in a linear fashion over time, the solution to the resultant integral equation involves adding one other term to the estimation model, ΔX, with the following addition to Equation (2.17):

$$\frac{c_1}{c_2}\left[\frac{e^{c_2 \Delta t} - 1}{c_2 \Delta t} - 1\right]\Delta X. \tag{2.21}$$

The quantity before the ΔX in this equation will be the regression coefficient β_3 from a regression model predicting Y_t from Y_{t-1}, X_{t-1}, and ΔX.

Provided that there are no feedback effects from Y to X and the error term is well-behaved, this model also can be estimated with OLS methods. For the party identification example, the results of this estimation are

$$\text{THERM}_2 = \tag{2.22}$$

	-1.61	$+$	$4.33\,\text{PID}_1$	$+$	$.64\,\text{THERM}_1$	$+$	$3.27\,\Delta\text{PID}$
	$(-.97)$		$(.23)$		$(.03)$		$(.96)$
			$\underline{.63}$		$\underline{.23}$		$\underline{.08}$

with standard errors in parentheses, standardized coefficients underscored, and an R^2 value of .59. Converting the OLS coefficients into the c parameters of the differential equation proceeds by first estimating c_2 from the β_2 coefficient according to Equation (2.19) above, and using the two other regression effects to generate two estimates of c_1, the effect of PID: one from the β_1 coefficient as in Equation (2.19) and one from the β_3 coefficient as

$$c_1 = \frac{\beta_3 c_2^2 \Delta t}{\beta_2 - 1 - \ln \beta_2}. \tag{2.23}$$

In the present instance, the estimate of c_1 from the β_1 coefficient yields a value of 1.79, and the estimate from the β_3 coefficient yields a value of 2.57. In either case, the estimates show that the 1.53 coefficient obtained earlier under the assumption that the exogenous variable did not change underestimated the true effect of party identification on the instantaneous rate of change of candidate ratings. Tuma and Hannan (1984) discuss various ways of combining the two values to produce the best estimate of c_1 from the data, ranging from a simple arithmetic average to pooled maximum likelihood methods.[7] Thus the two regression coefficients corresponding to X_{t-1} and ΔX in the continuous time model are used to provide a single estimate of the "continuously instantaneous" effect of X on Y.

Problems in the Estimation of Panel Models

The foregoing discussion may appear to imply that causal inference in the panel context is simply a matter of specifying continuous or discrete time static-score models, estimating causal effects through OLS regression, and interpreting the effects in terms of the influence of X on Y, or ΔY, controlling for Y_{t-1}. However, several obstacles to successful causal inference exist in the estimation of even the most basic static-score equation, and these potential problems will often render ordinary least squares regression inappropriate as the estimation procedure for panel analysis. The most important problems stem from the following possible errors in model specification:

1. *Reciprocal Causality.* If X_t and Y_t affect each other in a reciprocal causal system, then OLS will produce biased and inconsistent parameter estimates, and alternative estimators will need to be found that make use of additional variables and/or additional waves of observations in the panel.

2. *Measurement Error.* If Y_{t-1} is imperfectly measured, then its substantive effect on Y_t will not be estimated properly, nor will it serve as an appropriate control for the usual negative relationship between initial levels of Y and subsequent change. Indeed, as was discussed above, the measurement error in Y_{t-1} is one possible source of the negative correlation between Y_{t-1} and ΔY; but correcting for the problem by including Y_{t-1} directly in the model introduces bias as well because of the problems

associated with statistical estimation in the presence of error-laden independent variables. This bias often leads to the underestimation of the true effect of Y_{t-1} on Y_t, and to the overestimation of the estimated effects of the other explanatory variables.

3. *Omitted Variables and Autocorrelated Disturbances.* Finally, omitted variables can lead to several kinds of biases in panel models. Aside from the usual specification bias that may result from an omitted variable's correlation with observed independent variables, omitted variables in panel models may lead to *autocorrelation* in the endogenous variable's error terms over time. This in turn produces a nonzero correlation between Y_{t-1} and ϵ_t, yielding inconsistent OLS estimates of the effects of Y_{t-1} on Y_t in the static-score model. If the other independent variables are related to Y_{t-1}, autocorrelated disturbances may bias the estimates of their effects on Y_t as well.

These issues in the specification and estimation of static-score panel models will occupy the discussion for the remainder of the monograph. Although all of these problems present serious obstacles to successful causal inference, it will be seen that panel data often provide enough information to estimate parameters successfully in the face of these difficulties. In addition, many of these problems are endemic in *all* empirical research, and it will be shown that panel data provide the researcher with far greater ability to control these problems than is attained in cross-sectional analyses.

3. MODELS OF RECIPROCAL CAUSATION

The models in the previous chapter all contained the assumption that the relationship between X and Y was unidirectional, that is, that X influenced Y but not the reverse. In some instances, this assumption is entirely appropriate. For example, in models of the effects of race or other ascribed characteristics on an individual's income over time, or in research that models the effects of early adult experiences on later political or social orientations, the temporal (and hence potential causal) ordering between variables is clear. In other cases, theoretical reasons might preclude the testing of reciprocal causation, as, for example, in research that attempts to model the effects of economic indicators on government popularity in a set of countries observed over time. In these models, X_t, X_{t-1}, and/or ΔX

can be treated as exogenous variables in their respective equations, and parameter estimates can be obtained through OLS regression or, if the assumptions of no measurement error or autocorrelated disturbances cannot be justified, through procedures that will be discussed in later chapters.

But in many analyses, the assumption of unidirectional causality is not tenable, and indeed one of the primary motivations for analyzing panel data is to attempt to determine the causal ordering between the variables of interest. For example, we hypothesized in the previous chapter that group memberships influence an individual's behavioral orientation to protest, and that individuals' long-standing party attachments determine their feelings about presidential candidates during an election campaign; but theories of participation and group mobilization suggest that participation in protest activities may lead individuals to join more groups with a protest orientation, and theories of political partisanship suggest that attitudes about political candidates might alter individuals' long-term party loyalties as well. In these cases, theoretical concerns lead to plausible expectations of reciprocal causal relationships between X and Y.

Panel data offer decided advantages over cross-sectional analyses in testing for potential reciprocal causal effects between variables. Because cross-sectional data are collected at a single point in time, reciprocal effects models can be specified only with synchronous, or simultaneous, causal influences from one variable to the other, and the estimation of reciprocal causal effects would proceed by incorporating outside variables in an "instrumental variables" or Two Stage Least Squares analysis (Berry, 1984). However, the success of these methods depends, as we will see below, on the model satisfying several restrictive assumptions about the relationship of these outside variables with X, Y, and the disturbance terms of their respective equations. As shown in Chapter 2, the temporal component of panel designs allows the researcher to estimate models with lagged causal effects, where prior values of X influence future values of Y (or the change in Y), and vice versa. Further, models with reciprocal simultaneous or synchronous causal effects may be identified and estimated under certain conditions without making the possibly dubious assumptions about the effects of outside instrumental variables that are necessary in cross-sectional research.

This chapter outlines the uses of panel data in assisting in causal inference in models with reciprocal effects between variables. It will be emphasized that panel designs are a powerful means of estimating reciprocal causal effects, although they offer no automatic method for "proving causality." The estimation of reciprocal effects always takes place within the context of particular hypothesized models, and the assumptions contained in these models must be defended in a given situation. In particular, two-wave reciprocal effects models involve a set of possibly restrictive assumptions that can be relaxed only, as in cross-sectional research, by including outside variables. Three-wave and multiwave panels, however, can be estimated by imposing fewer constraints on the causal parameters.

Cross-Lagged Effects Models

The Two-Wave Model

The most basic model for estimating possible reciprocal effects is an extension to two dependent variables of the lagged effect static-score model considered in the previous chapter (Equation 2.14), with each variable at time 2 being predicted by its previous value as well as the time 1 value of the other variable of interest. This model is shown in diagram form in Figure 3.1. X_1 and X_2 represent one variable (e.g., group memberships) measured across the two panel waves, and Y_1 and Y_2 another variable (e.g., protest potential) measured at both time points. X_2 and Y_2 are hypothesized to be determined by their wave 1 values, the lagged value of the other variable, and an error term U. The correlation between the wave 1 variables is represented in the figure by ρ_1, and the correlation between the structural disturbances of the wave 2 equations is represented by $\rho_{U_1 U_2}$. The two structural equations can be written as follows:

$$Y_2 = \beta_1 X_1 + \beta_2 Y_1 + U_1$$
$$X_2 = \beta_3 Y_1 + \beta_4 X_1 + U_2$$

(3.1)

with all variables in the model expressed in mean deviation form to eliminate consideration of the intercept term.

The cross-lagged model has wide applicability in panel analysis. When change in the dependent variables is modeled according to a discrete time process, the cross-lagged model will be appropriate whenever the causal lags are approximately equal to the time period between measurements. When change in the dependent variables occur continuously, it can be shown that the cross-lagged model represents the integral solution to a system of differential equations where the instantaneous rates of change in X and Y are dependent on one another over time, as in

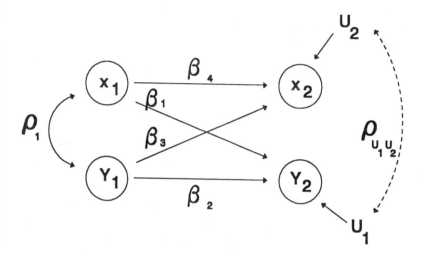

Figure 3.1. Two-Wave Model With Cross-Lagged Effects

$$\frac{dY_t}{dt} = c_0 + c_1 X_t + c_2 Y_t$$

$$\frac{dX_t}{dt} = c_3 + c_4 Y_t + c_5 X_t .$$

$$(3.2)$$

The β_k in Equation (3.1) are, as in the single-equation continuous time model considered in the previous chapter, nonlinear functions of the c coefficients, the "fundamental parameters of change" in Equation (3.2), and the time between panel waves. The calculation of the c coefficients from the β_k involves complex mathematical manipulations beyond the scope of this monograph; interested readers are referred to Arminger (1986), Coleman (1968, pp. 448-452), and Tuma and Hannan (1984, Chapters 11-12) for details. For our purposes, it is sufficient to note that when the causal system is one of continuous reciprocal feedback from one variable to another, the cross-lagged model "tends not to be misleading about the *direction* of causal influence" (Dwyer, 1983, p. 352).

It may also be noted that the cross-lagged model corresponds to the so-called "Granger test" for causality in time series analysis, which posits that a variable "Granger-causes" the other if any value of the first variable measured at times $t - 1$, $t - 2$, and so on, has a significant effect on the second variable at time t, controlling for all of the second variable's prior values (Gujarati, 1988, pp. 542-543). In the two-wave case, this reduces to the model of Equation (3.1), whereas in multiwave panel data, this results in a cross-lagged model predicting each Y and X at time t with Y and X at times $t - 1$, $t - 2$, and so on.

Estimation of the Cross-Lagged Model

Originally, it was argued that the causal direction between variables could be ascertained through this model by comparing the *cross-lagged correlations* between the two variables, that is, $\rho_{X_1 Y_2}$ and $\rho_{Y_1 X_2}$. If the causal effect from the variable represented by X_1 and X_2 on the variable represented by Y_1 and Y_2 was of greater magnitude than the effect in the opposite direction, then it was argued that $\rho_{X_1 Y_2}$ would be larger than $\rho_{Y_1 X_2}$. As numerous scholars subsequently demonstrated, however, this reasoning is fallacious because the cross-lagged correlations between variables in Figure 3.1 are produced by several components:

$$\rho_{X_1 Y_2} = \beta_1 + \rho_1 \beta_2$$

$$\rho_{Y_1 X_2} = \beta_3 + \rho_1 \beta_4.$$

(3.3)

As can be seen, the cross-lagged correlation contains not only the causal effect between variables (β_1 and β_3) but also the stability of each variable over time and the intercorrelation of the two variables at wave 1. Thus the cross-lagged correlation of X_1 and Y_2 could be larger than that between X_2 and Y_1 even if β_3 was larger than β_1 if the stability of Y was greater than the stability of X over time (Markus, 1979, pp. 48-49). Because comparison of causal effects can be done only by recovering β_1 and β_3 directly, regression and structural equation methods have supplanted cross-lagged correlation analysis as a means of determining causal direction and strength. We shall see in Chapter 5, however, that comparison of cross-lagged correlations does have some utility for the panel analyst in testing certain restrictive models of spurious association between variables.

Under the assumptions that the disturbance terms U have means of zero, constant variance, and are uncorrelated with the lagged endogenous variables X_1 and Y_1, the cross-lagged model's parameters may be estimated consistently through ordinary least squares regression. As noted above, the coefficients of particular interest in this model are the cross-lagged effects from the wave 1 variables X_1 and Y_1 to Y_2 and X_2, respectively, because these are presumed to represent the causal effect from each variable to the other. In the language of change scores discussed in the previous chapter, the effect of X_1 on Y_2, controlling for Y_1, represents the effect of X_1 on the *changes* in Y over time, and the same interpretation holds for the effect of Y_1 on X_2, controlling for X_1. Examination of the R^2 values for the X_2 and Y_2 equations shows the extent to which the lagged variables explain the variance in the dependent variables, and the correlation of the error terms U_1 and U_2 represents covariation between X_2 and Y_2 that is not accounted for by the cross-lagged (or continuous time) causal process and the stability effects specified in the model.

This procedure is illustrated by extending the analysis from Chapter 2 of legal political protest potential with individual group memberships in Germany. Earlier it was assumed that the direction of causality between protest and group memberships was unidirectional; the results from estimating the cross-lagged model in Figure 3.1 show that both variables have significant effects on one another. The OLS regression estimates of this model (unstandardized coefficients, standard errors in parentheses, standardized coefficients underscored) are

$$\text{PROTEST}_2 = \quad .22 \quad + \quad \underset{\substack{(.02) \\ \underline{.11}}}{.04\ \text{GROUPS}_1} \quad + \quad \underset{\substack{(.05) \\ \underline{.47}}}{.47\ \text{PROTEST}_1} \quad (3.4)$$

with an adjusted R^2 value of .28, and

$$\text{GROUPS}_2 = \quad .01 \quad + \quad \underset{\substack{(.14) \\ \underline{.20}}}{.58\ \text{PROTEST}_1} \quad + \quad \underset{\substack{(.05) \\ \underline{.42}}}{.46\ \text{GROUPS}_1}$$

with an R^2 value also of .29. All coefficients in both equations are statistically significant. The results show that, according to this model, membership in protest-encouraging groups at wave 1 affects changes in protest potential between the two waves, and protest potential at wave 1 significantly affects changes in memberships in groups that encourage protest between waves 1 and 2 as well. In fact, in this model the effects from protest to group memberships are approximately twice as large in magnitude as the opposite causal effect that was the focus in Chapter 2. The correlation between structural disturbances for the two endogenous variables is .22, which, compared to the observed .46 correlation between PROTEST and GROUPS in 1989, suggests that about half of the observed relationship between the two variables is accounted for by the stabilities and cross-lagged effects specified in the model. Other factors, possibly including synchronous causal effects and/or joint relationships with omitted outside variables, account for the remaining covariation between X_2 and Y_2.

Three-Wave and Multiwave Cross-Lagged Models

When three or more waves of data are available, the cross-lagged model can be estimated for each time period ($t > 1$) separately using the procedures just discussed. A more common approach, however, is to estimate the parameters in the entire model simultaneously using LISREL or a related structural equation package, as these techniques can be extended to handle more complex models with measurement error and autocorrelated disturbances, provide information about the relative fit of the model compared with alternative specifications, and allow constraints to be placed on coefficients in order to estimate theoretical effects of interest.

For example, three waves of data are available with which to model a possible reciprocal causal relationship between party identification (X) and evaluations of presidential candidates (Y) during the 1980 campaign. Following our earlier discussion, if we assume that the reciprocal effects between these variables operate *continuously* during the campaign, the parameters in the resulting system of differential equations depicted in Equation (3.2) may be recovered through estimation of the cross-lagged model. We show the three-wave cross-lagged model in Figure 3.2, using LISREL notation for expository purposes (see Appendix).

Party identification at wave 1 (February 1980), 2 (June), and 3 (September) are depicted in the figure as endogenous variables η_1, η_2, and η_3, and the candidate thermometer score is depicted as η_4, η_5, and η_6. η_1 and η_4 are actually predetermined variables but here we treat them as endogenous variables that are completely determined by their error terms so that all causal effects between variables will be in LISREL's **B** matrix of coefficients linking endogenous variables. This specification has no bearing on any substantive conclusion, but it is necessary so that equality constraints may be placed on the β_k across waves, as will be discussed below. There are only two relevant matrices in the LISREL setup for this model: the **B** matrix, and the **Ψ** matrix of the variances and covariances between the ζ_k, the structural disturbances of the endogenous variables. The ψ_{41} covariance between ζ_1 and ζ_4 represents the wave 1 covariance between variables η_1

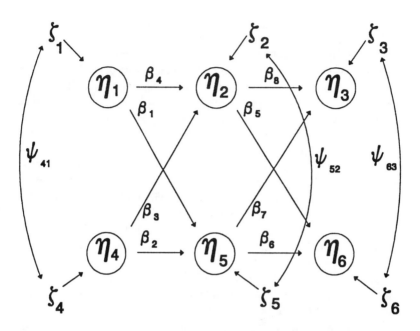

Figure 3.2. Three-Wave Cross-Lagged Model With LISREL Notation

and η_4, and the ψ covariances between ζ_2 and ζ_5, and between ζ_3 and ζ_6, represent the covariation between party identification and candidate ratings that cannot be explained at waves 2 and 3 through the continuous time reciprocal effects process specified in the model.

As discussed above, the β_k in continuous time models are nonlinear functions of the effects of the variables on X and Y's instantaneous rates of change and the time period between panel measurements. Consequently, if the panel waves are equally spaced, then the β_k should also be equal across waves, so that the cross-lagged effects between variables from wave 1 to wave 2 should be equal to their values from wave 2 to wave 3, as should the estimates of each variable's stability. The model then can be estimated by placing the following *consistency*, or *equality constraints*, on the parameters: $\beta_1 = \beta_5$, $\beta_2 = \beta_6$, $\beta_3 = \beta_7$, $\beta_4 = \beta_8$. The assumption of constant effects can be tested by relaxing these constraints and comparing the fit of the two models. If the time period between waves of observation is unequal, then the constraints on the β_k will be nonlinear across waves, rather than simple equalities (Arminger, 1987, p. 343). The specification of nonlinear constraints on parameters across waves is difficult, although not impossible, within the LISREL framework, and the reader is referred to Hayduk (1987) and Rindskopf (1984) for applications of these methods.

In the present example, we assume constancy of structural effects for illustrative purposes, although the time period between waves 1 and 2 is approximately 1 month longer than that between waves 2 and 3. We also assume that $\psi_{52} = \psi_{63}$, that is, that the covariance between disturbances of the party identification and candidate ratings in wave 2 is equal to their covariation in wave 3. All other disturbance covariances (aside from ψ_{41}) are assumed to be zero, which in this model amounts to the assumption that there is no autocorrelation of disturbance terms. These assumptions may also be relaxed and tested against the data, as will be shown in more detail in Chapter 5. Given these constraints placed on the structural parameters and disturbance terms, the model is overidentified with 9 degrees of freedom. The results of LISREL maximum likelihood estimates of this model are shown in Table 3.1.

The results show statistically significant reciprocal causal effects between party identification and candidate ratings. The standardized effect from party identification to candidate ratings is approximately twice as large as the effect in the opposite direction. The stability of both party identification and candidate ratings is quite high, and the small values obtained for the standardized ψ covariance between the disturbances for party and candidate ratings at waves 2 and 3 suggest that the model accounts very well for the synchronous covariation between these two variables.

It can be seen, however, that the model fits the data quite poorly, as shown by the χ^2 value of 201.1 with 9 degrees of freedom. Relaxing the assumption of equality between structural parameters across waves and equality between the party and candidate ratings disturbance covariation for waves 2 and 3 yields almost identical estimates of structural effects, and a χ^2 value of 190.2 with 4 degrees of freedom. Because the first model is "nested" within the second, the difference between the two χ^2 values also follows a χ^2 distribution, and in this case the χ^2 difference of 10.9 with 5 degrees of freedom difference indicates that a model without equality constraints *does not* represent a statistically significant improvement in fit to the data. At the same time, further modifications in the model should be made because of the poor overall fit; we will consider models that relax the assumptions of no measurement error and no autocorrelation of structural disturbances in subsequent chapters.

TABLE 3.1
Three-Wave Cross-Lagged Effects Model:
Party Identification and Candidate Evaluations, 1980

Stability Effects	
Candidate Evaluations	
β_2	.67[a]
	.62
β_6	.67[a]
	.64
Party Identification	
β_4	.83[b]
	.82
β_8	.83[b]
	.83
Cross-Lagged Effects	
Party to Candidate	
β_1	3.98[c]
	.21
β_5	3.98[c]
	.21
Candidate to Party	
β_3	.01[d]
	.08
β_7	.01[d]
	.09
Error Covariances	
ψ_{41}	29.58
	.44
ψ_{52}	4.45[e]
	.06
ψ_{63}	4.45[e]
	.06
R^2 (η_2) Candidate Evaluation, Wave 2	.54
R^2 (η_3) Candidate Evaluation, Wave 3	.58
R^2 (η_5) Party Identification, Wave 2	.73
R^2 (η_6) Party Identification, Wave 3	.77
χ^2 (df)	201.1 (9)

SOURCE: American National Election Study, Major Panel File, 1980.
NOTE: Unstandardized maximum likelihood coefficients; standardized coefficients underscored. All coefficients statistically significant.
a, b, c, d, e. Coefficients constrained to be equal.

Synchronous Effects Models

The relative simplicity of the estimation procedures for the cross-lagged model undoubtedly has contributed to its popularity as a means for untangling causal interrelationships. But recall from the previous chapter that these models' assumption that synchronous or cotemporal effects between variables are zero (i.e., that the causal effects between variables result only from the impact of the *lagged* variables X_1 and Y_1) may not be tenable in many research situations. In panel models with long time periods between the waves of measurement relative to the true causal lags, estimation of only the cross-lagged effect will not capture the full causal influence of each variable on the other. In some models, moreover, the assumption of cross-lagged effects is literally impossible, as in Dwyer's example (1983, p. 393) of reciprocal effects exerted by new college roommates on one another's moods. The presence of cotemporal or synchronous influences between variables necessitates alternative methods of estimating the reciprocal causal effects.

In some instances, the appropriate causal model will contain *only* synchronous reciprocal effects between variables at a given time point. In other cases, there may be both cotemporal effects and cross-lagged effects between variables, as the lag values will account for some but not all of a variable's causal influence. As might be expected, models that include both lagged and cotemporal effects present some special problems in identification and estimation, and will be discussed after the more straightforward synchronous effects model. This model is shown for the two-wave case in diagram form as Figure 3.3, and as the following system of equations:

$$Y_2 = \beta_1 Y_1 + \beta_3 X_2 + U_1$$

$$X_2 = \beta_2 X_1 + \beta_4 Y_2 + U_2.$$

(3.5)

The reciprocal effects specified between X_2 and Y_2 mean that the model is nonrecursive and poses problems for OLS estimation (Berry, 1984). Because X_2 is related to U_1 (via the latter's indirect effect through Y_2), and Y_2 similarly is related to U_2, the assumption in OLS that the independent variables are unrelated to the disturbance term for the dependent variable necessarily will be violated (if β_3 and β_4 do not equal zero in the population). Hence OLS estimation will yield biased estimates of the causal parameters in the model. Further, in many nonrecursive models the parame-

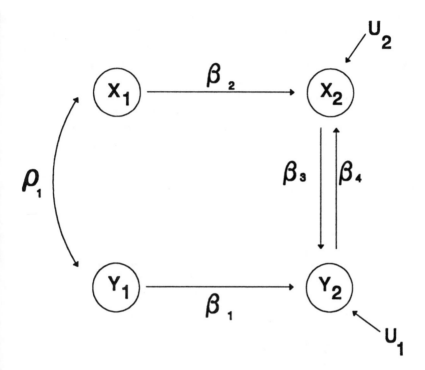

Figure 3.3. Two-Wave Model With Synchronous Effects

ters are not identified, and so we will need to verify that enough information exists in the form of observed variances and covariances to estimate the coefficients of interest.

In order to identify and estimate the Y_2 equation, the model must contain one or more "instrumental variables" that satisfy the following conditions: (a) it is related to X_2 but uncorrelated with U_1 and (b) it has no direct causal effect on Y_2. In order to identify and estimate the X_2 equation, at least one instrumental variable is needed that is related to Y_2 but uncorrelated with U_2, and that has no direct causal effect on X_2. Under the assumptions of the present model, the lagged variables X_1 and Y_1 fulfill both conditions. Because they are assumed to be predetermined variables, they are by definition uncorrelated with the disturbance terms of both equations; and because this model assumes that both cross-lagged effects are zero, the second condition is fulfilled as well. Consequently, both equations satisfy the order condition and are just-identified: One exogenous (technically, predetermined) variable is excluded from each equation that has one endogenous variable as a predictor. This utilization of the lagged dependent variable to estimate reciprocal effects is one of the major putative advantages of panel analysis; however, it should be noted that the procedure is valid only under the potentially restrictive assumptions of no cross-lagged effects and no autocorrelation between the error terms of equations in consecutive panel waves. If either of these assumptions do not hold, X_1 and Y_1 may no longer be used to identify, respectively, the Y_2 and X_2 equations (Berry, 1984).

Estimation and Evaluation of the Synchronous Effects Model

Because each parameter in the synchronous effects model is just-identified, their values may be estimated through algebraic manipulation of the model's four "normal" equations, that is, the predicted covariances between the two endogenous variables Y_2 and X_2 and each exogenous variable Y_1 and X_1. The normal equations are obtained by multiplying the equations for the two endogenous variables by each exogenous variable, summing across all cases, and taking expectations to yield

$$\text{Cov}(X_1 X_2) = \beta_2 \text{Var}(X_1) + \beta_4 \text{Cov}(X_1 Y_2)$$

$$\text{Cov}(Y_1 X_2) = \beta_2 \text{Cov}(X_1 Y_1) + \beta_4 \text{Cov}(Y_1 Y_2)$$

$$\tag{3.6}$$

$$\text{Cov}(X_1 Y_2) = \beta_1 \text{Cov}(X_1 Y_1) + \beta_3 \text{Cov}(X_1 X_2)$$

$$\text{Cov}(Y_1 Y_2) = \beta_1 \text{Var}(Y_1) + \beta_3 \text{Cov}(Y_1 X_2).$$

β_2 and β_4 are obtained through manipulation of the first two normal equations, and β_1 and β_3 through manipulation of the last two.

Equivalently, these parameters can be estimated from sample data through the statistical procedure known as Two Stage Least Squares (TSLS). Estimates may also be obtained through LISREL maximum likelihood or related procedures, but we explicate the logic of instrumental variable models by focusing here on Two Stage Least Squares. For the Y_2 equation, the TSLS procedure begins by regressing X_2 on its instrumental variable X_1 (or set of instrumental variables) and all other predetermined variables in the model to yield

$$\hat{X}_2 = \beta_0 + \beta_1 Y_1 + \beta_2 X_1 . \tag{3.7}$$

Note that *all* predetermined (exogenous) variables, even those such as Y_1 that subsequently cause Y_2 but are not specifically modeled as causes of X_2, are used in this first-stage equation. The goal is to obtain the best possible estimate of X_2 because the standard errors of the coefficients in the second-stage equation depend directly on the precision of the estimates in the first stage (Berry, 1984). This is another advantage of the use of lagged variables as instruments, because Y_1 and X_1 are likely to have stronger correlations with their time 2 values than other potential exogenous variables. The estimate of X_2 is now uncorrelated with the error term U_1 because it is a linear combination of predetermined variables that, by definition, are uncorrelated with all error terms in the model. The second stage of the procedure substitutes the surrogate $\hat{X}_2$ into Equation (3.5), and all coefficients and associated standard errors may be estimated consistently with OLS. A similar two-stage process is used to generate consistent estimates of the parameters in the X_2 equation in (3.5): Regress Y_2 on its instrument Y_1 and X_1, the other predetermined variable, to generate a $\hat{Y}_2$ that is uncorrelated with U_2, and then regress X_2 on $\hat{Y}_2$ and X_1 in the second stage. The assumptions discussed above, that X_1 has no direct effect on Y_2 and that Y_1 has no direct effect on X_2, are essential here because otherwise each equation would be underidentified: $\hat{X}_2$ and $\hat{Y}_2$ would then be linear combinations of all the other independent variables in their respective equations in (3.5) and no unique estimates of causal effects could be obtained.

Although it is possible to conduct these analyses in two separate steps, statistical software programs now usually contain a Two Stage Least Squares procedure that estimates the coefficients from both steps simultaneously. The advantage of using these routines, aside from computational convenience, is that they provide the correct standard errors, standardized coefficients, and R^2 estimates for the second-stage equation, in that the statistics are calculated based on the original, not predicted, values of X_2 and Y_2 (Berry, 1984, pp. 68-69). Following these procedures with the protest potential and group membership example from the West German panel study yields estimates of

$$\text{PROTEST}_2 = \quad .22 \quad + \quad .09 \ \text{GROUPS}_2 \quad + \quad .42 \ \text{PROTEST}_1 \tag{3.8}$$
$$(.04) \qquad\qquad\qquad (.06)$$
$$\underline{.26} \qquad\qquad\qquad \underline{.42}$$

with an R^2 value of .30, and

$$\text{GROUPS}_2 = \quad -.27 \quad + \quad \underset{(.29)}{\underset{.42}{1.24}} \text{ PROTEST}_2 + \underset{(.05)}{\underset{.37}{.41}} \text{ GROUPS}_1$$

also with an R^2 value of .30. As in the cross-lagged model, all coefficients in both equations are statistically significant.

At first glance, the synchronous effects model appears to be superior to the cross-lagged model estimated earlier. The explained variances of both dependent variables are larger, and stronger reciprocal causal effects appear to exist between protest and group memberships. However, an attractive feature of the synchronous effects model is that 1 degree of freedom exists with which to test an important assumption of the model. Although we saw above that each of the parameters in the synchronous effects model is just-identified, the model as a whole has 1 degree of freedom, as there are 10 observed variances and covariances and only 9 parameters to be estimated (the four β, two variances of the U, the variances of X_1 and Y_1, and their covariance ρ_1). This degree of freedom can be used to test that the model's specification of zero covariance between the disturbances of the endogenous variables is accurate, that is, $\rho_{U_1 U_2} = 0$. This specification of zero residual covariance implies that the synchronous effects and stabilities of the variables in the model completely account for the observed covariance between X_2 and Y_2. In the present example, the predicted covariance between U_1 and U_2 is $-.05$, with a standardized value of $-.45$, a relatively large and substantively implausible value.[8]

Although it is not impossible for negative covariation to exist between the disturbance terms in synchronous effects panel models, the interpretation of such a finding is somewhat problematic. What it indicates is that some outside factor is positively influencing one of the two (positively) reciprocally related endogenous variables and negatively influencing the other. These factors are often difficult to imagine, leading to the more likely interpretation that the model is misspecified. Gillespie and Fox (1980) show that estimates of negative covariances between disturbances in many synchronous effects models may be associated with several types of model misspecification, among them measurement error in the endogenous or exogenous variables, the exclusion of cross-lagged effects, and the omission of variables that influence both the exogenous and endogenous variables, which in the panel context would indicate autocorrelated disturbances for variables over time. Aside from measurement error in the endogenous variables, each of these misspecifications results in an upward bias in the calculation of the reciprocal synchronous effects. If not for the "correction" represented by the negative covariation between the residuals, the model would overpredict the covariation between the endogenous variables.[9] Thus the finding of positive reciprocal effects in the synchronous model may well be an artifact of model misspecification if the residual covariance has a large negative value. Under these conditions, cross-lagged effects could be added to the model as described below, and/or models could be estimated following procedures discussed in later chapters that test for the possible biases produced by measurement error and omitted variables.

Cross-Lagged and Synchronous Effects Models

If there are no compelling theoretical reasons to estimate models with either exclusive cross-lagged or exclusive synchronous effects, or if a synchronous model yields implausible or uninterpretable results, a model including both types of effects is a reasonable alternative specification. However, the addition of cross-lagged effects from Y_1 to X_2 and from X_1 to Y_2 in Figure 3.3 results in a model with 11 free parameters and only 10 observed variances and covariances. The model as a whole, as well as each individual parameter, is underidentified. The solution to the identification problem was solved for the cross-lagged model by constraining the synchronous effects to be zero; likewise the constraint that the cross-lagged effects were zero identified the parameters in the synchronous model. When both types of effects are assumed to be present, identification must be achieved through additional information, either in the form of outside variables or more waves of information.

The Two-Wave Model

When only two waves of data are available, the only means of identifying the model is to include outside exogenous variables and constrain some of their effects to be zero. In order to identify the Y_2 equation, at least one outside variable (Z_1) must be included that satisfies the above conditions for instrumental variable analysis: (a) it must have a direct causal effect on X_2 but *no* direct causal effect on Y_2 and (b) it must be exogenous and therefore uncorrelated with either U_1 or U_2. At least one additional outside variable (Z_2) must be included to identify the X_2 equation that is also exogenous, and it must have a direct effect on Y_2 but no effect on X_2. As might be imagined, such variables are difficult to find, especially when conducting secondary analysis of panel data where these types of instrumental variables were not measured by design. Further, the outside variables must be fairly strongly linked to the endogenous variables in order to increase the efficiency of the second-stage estimates. The researcher cannot impose the constraints on the outside variables arbitrarily simply to achieve identification, as the resultant estimates will be biased to the extent that the instrumental variables violate the necessary assumptions. Instrumental variables that are derived from theoretical considerations are the ideal. In other instances, logical reasons will allow the specification of certain relationships, as in Jennings and Niemi's (1975) specification of parental party identification as an instrument for each spouse's own partisanship in a reciprocal effects model. It is unreasonable to assume, for example, that a wife's parent's party identification has a direct causal influence on a husband's partisanship, and vice versa.

In practice, panel analysts using individual-level data typically will use social background variables such as education or age as instruments, because often they may be considered as fixed exogenous variables and hence unrelated to the disturbances. However, if these variables do not have strong effects on X_2 or Y_2 in the first-stage equation, then the standard errors of all coefficients in the second-stage equation will be relatively imprecise. Further, if the Z variable used as an instrument for Y_2 actually has a direct effect on X_2, then the second-stage equation would be misspecified and biased parameter estimates would be obtained. In this regard, the ideal situation is to build instrumental variables into the design of a panel study, where exogenous variables can be specified in advance that will have a relatively powerful effect on either X_2 or Y_2 yet be unrelated to the disturbance terms of their equations.

The combined cross-lagged and synchronous model with appropriate instruments may be estimated either through Two Stage Least Squares or within the LISREL framework with maximum likelihood methods. The TSLS estimation proceeds as above: To obtain the coefficients in the Y_2 equation, regress X_2 on X_1, Y_1, and Z_1 to generate $\hat{X}_2$, and then regress Y_2 on Y_1, X_1, and $\hat{X}_2$; to obtain the coefficients in the X_2 equation, regress Y_2 on Y_1, X_1, and Z_2 to generate $\hat{Y}_2$, and then regress X_2 on Y_1, X_1, and $\hat{Y}_2$. As in the earlier example, it is recommended that a TSLS procedure in an existing software package be used to estimate correctly the structural coefficients and associated statistics of the model.

The specification of the LISREL matrices for maximum likelihood estimation is straightforward. X_1, Y_1, Z_1, and Z_2 can be specified as exogenous ξ variables, and X_2 and Y_2 are the endogenous variables η_1 and η_2.

The effects from the time 1 variables and the Z are specified in the Γ matrix linking exogenous to endogenous variables, with individual γ elements constrained to be zero according to the hypothesized role of the instrumental variables in the causal system. In this case, the γ effects from Z_1 to Y_2 and from Z_2 to X_2 would be constrained to be zero. To complete the causal specifications, both off-diagonal elements of $\mathbf{B}$ are freed to represent the reciprocal effects of X and Y at time 2. As there are 21 observed variances and covariances and 20 free parameters (10 elements of the $\boldsymbol{\Phi}$ variance-covariance matrix of exogenous variables, 2 β, 6 γ, and 2 ψ disturbance variances for the time 2 variables), there is 1 degree of freedom remaining in the model. As discussed above, this degree of freedom tests the constraint that the covariance between the structural disturbances U_1 and U_2 is zero.

One potential problem in the estimation of these types of models is multicollinearity between the cross-lagged and synchronous effects. Depending on the effects of the instrumental variables, the magnitude of the causal effects, and the degree of stability in the variables over time, it may not be possible to obtain precise estimates of both the cross-lagged and synchronous causal effects. If multicollinearity is severe, based on examination of the standard errors and correlations between parameter estimates, then it may only be possible to test for the *joint* effect of both independent variables on a particular dependent variable. A model constraining both the cross-lagged and synchronous effects of, for example, group memberships on protest potential to be zero is nested within the model that includes both effects. If Two Stage Least Squares is used to estimate coefficients, then a nested F test may be conducted to determine whether the unconstrained model has significantly more explanatory power than the constrained model. In LISREL, the difference in χ^2 values, given the differences in the models' degrees of freedom, provides a test of whether the unconstrained model better accounts for the observed data than the constrained model with no causal effects. The researcher may then determine that one variable's cross-lagged and synchronous effects on the other are jointly significant. Mayer and Carroll (1987) outline some further χ^2 difference tests for determining whether all cross-lagged, all synchronous, or all causal effects between variables aside from their stabilities are statistically significant as well.

The procedures outlined here summarize the available means for estimating the coefficients of two-wave reciprocal effects models. When strong theoretical reasons exist for assuming a certain lag structure, either the synchronous or cross-lagged effects are set to zero, and the model is identified in both cases. When the analyst has no strong a priori reason to exclude one category of effects or another, models that include both may be identified and estimated only after including outside variables and imposing restrictions on their causal effects. If the model does not fit the data, however, relaxing the restrictions results in an underidentified model; and, if autocorrelated disturbances are suspected, then additional instrumental variables will be necessary for estimation. In many instances, therefore, two-wave analysis will provide inconclusive results, and three-wave or multiwave data will need to be analyzed.

The Three-Wave Model

If three or more waves of data are available, models with both cross-lagged and synchronous effects may be estimated with greater flexibility in the imposition and testing of various constraints on the causal parameters. One possibility is to specify cross-lagged and synchronous effects between the time 2 and time 3 variables of interest, and then use the time 1 values as instruments in the TSLS or maximum likelihood procedure as above. But in the event that there is no direct effect of X_1 on X_3, controlling for X_2 (or Y_1 on Y_3, controlling for Y_2), the instrumental variable approach will break down. Further, the model does not provide an accurate depiction of the causal processes across time because it ignores all causal interrelationships between wave 1 and wave 2 variables.

Alternatively, the three-wave model can be estimated by extending the LISREL cross-lagged model of Figure 3.2 and imposing additional restrictions on parameter values. We may add the following parameters to the model of Figure 3.2 to represent the full cross-lagged and synchronous specification: β_9 and β_{11} to represent the synchronous effect of one variable on the other at times 2 and 3, and β_{10} and β_{12} to represent the time 2 and 3 effect in the reverse direction. The model as a whole has 2 degrees of freedom, as there are 21 variances and covariances of the six observed variables, and 19 free parameters to estimate—12 β parameters, 6 variances of the structural disturbances, and 1 covariance between the structural disturbances of the wave 1 variables. However, no individual equation for any wave 2 or 3 endogenous variable is identified, as in each case there are more endogenous variables in the prediction equation than omitted predetermined variables. Including outside predetermined variables and imposing certain restrictions on their causal effects is one possible strategy for identification but, as we have seen, these variables may not be available, or the assumptions underlying this procedure may not be defensible in a given situation. An alternative strategy is to identify the model by imposing *consistency constraints* on the parameters. Kessler and Greenberg (1981) show that imposing any two of the following restrictions achieves identification of the model, and imposing all three renders the model overidentified: $\beta_1 = \beta_5$, $\beta_2 = \beta_6$, $\beta_9 = \beta_{11}$. The first constraint sets the stability of one variable at adjacent waves to be equal, the second equates the cross-lagged effects of one variable on the other between waves 1 and 2 and waves 2 and 3, whereas the third equates the synchronous effects of one variable on the other at waves 2 and 3. It should be noted that it is necessary to impose the constraints on the determinants of only one of the variables; in the model above, if consistency constraints are placed on the parameters for the η_5 and η_6 equations, the parameters in the η_2 and η_3 equations may still be identified without constraint. However, in most cases there will be little theoretical justification for imposing constraints on the effects on one variable over the other, and the analyses could begin with a model that includes consistency constraints on the effects for both variables, with later models relaxing the constraints as appropriate. If more waves of data are available, the additional degrees of freedom provide enough information with which to estimate model parameters, including disturbance covariances, without many of the consistency constraints necessary in the three-wave case.

We test this model by using data from the National Youth Survey, a panel study of 1,725 American youths aged 12-17 that began in 1976. Interviews were conducted in each of the subsequent 4 years, although the analysis will be limited to the first 3 years (1976-1978) of the panel. The surveys contain measures of the youths' self-reported delinquent behavior, drug and alcohol usage, as well as numerous other variables that have been proposed to explain delinquency and drug abuse among youth in the psychological and sociological literature. We hypothesize that an individual's self-reported delinquent behavior is determined to some extent by his or her involvement with delinquent peers, and that delinquent behavior may also increase an individual's involvement with similarly oriented peers (see Elliott, Huizinga, & Ageton, 1985, and Menard & Elliott, 1990, for descriptions of the NYS surveys).

A general self-reported delinquency scale for each youth in 1976, 1977, and 1978 was constructed by averaging responses to six behavioral items asking the youths how often they had engaged in each activity during the previous year (from "0" for "never" to "6" for "two to three times a day"). An "involvement with delinquent peers" scale was constructed in each panel wave following the procedures outlined in Elliott et al. (1985) by multiplying together one index measuring the amount of time the youths spent with friends during afternoons, evenings, and weekends ("0" for "none" to "5" for "a great deal"), with another index measuring their perceptions of how many of their friends ("1" for "none of them" to "5" for "all of them") engage in six different delinquent activities.

The maximum likelihood estimates of parameters for several variants of this model are shown in Table 3.2. η_1 to η_3 represent involvement with delinquent peers (IDP) in 1976, 1977, and 1978, and η_4, η_5, and η_6 represent the respondent's self-reported delinquency (SRD) in the three panel waves. The first column of the table shows the results with consistency constraints imposed on the causal effects for both the SRD and IDP variables; that is, the model imposes the following equalities: $\beta_1 = \beta_5$, $\beta_2 = \beta_6$, $\beta_9 = \beta_{11}$, the restrictions for the SRD equations, and $\beta_4 = \beta_8$, $\beta_3 = \beta_7$, $\beta_{10} = \beta_{12}$, the restrictions for the IDP equations.

The model has 8 degrees of freedom and shows a poor fit to the data, as indicated by the χ^2 value. The substantive interpretation of the model, however, suggests that the causal interrelationships may follow what can be termed a "feedback" process (Plewis, 1985), where the variables influence one another at different lags. Here there are significant synchronous effects from IDP to SRD and significant lagged effects from SRD to IDP. Such a pattern makes sense substantively in this case, as association with delinquent peers influences one's own delinquency during the same time period, and delinquency then leads individuals to associate with peers with similar behavioral orientations in the following year.

The second column shows the reestimation of the model after omitting insignificant causal effects. This model (2) is nested within model (1) because it has the same parameter matrices except for the restriction in model (2) that β_1, β_5, β_{10}, and β_{12} are zero. We may then use the difference in χ^2 values to test whether model (1) represents a significant improvement in fit over model (2). Here the χ^2 difference is 1.3, which is insignificant, given the difference of 2 degrees of freedom between the models, leading to an acceptance of model (2) compared to model (1). Substantively, the effects indicate that the synchronous effect from IDP to SRD is approximately 50% larger than the lagged effect from SRD to IDP, with both sets of effects being of moderate magnitude.

Because the model without synchronous reciprocal effects is now fully recursive, we may relax the equality constraints that were imposed earlier to identify the model, and test these constraints through comparison of the model χ^2. The third column shows the results of this estimation and indicates that there is little improvement in model fit once the equality constraints are relaxed, nor are there any significant changes in the size of

TABLE 3.2

Three-Wave Reciprocal Effects Models: Self-Reported Delinquency and Involvement With Delinquent Peers, 1976-1978

	Model		
	(1)	(2)	(3)
Stability Effects			
SRD			
β_2	.40[a]	.37[a]	.35
	.41	.37	.36
β_6	.40[a]	.37[a]	.40
	.38	.35	.37
IDP			
β_4	.54[b]	.59[b]	.61
	.45	.49	.49
β_8	.54[b]	.59[b]	.56
	.48	.51	.51
Cross-Lagged Effects			
SRD to IDP			
β_3	2.83[c]	1.74[c]	1.67
	.37	.23	.22
β_7	2.83[c]	1.74[c]	1.75
	.42	.23	.26
IDP to SRD			
β_1	−.01[d]*	——	——
	−.05		
β_5	−.01[d]*	——	——
	−.05		
Synchronous Effects			
SRD to IDP			
β_{10}	−1.58[e]*	——	——
	−.25		
β_{12}	−1.58[e]*	——	——
	−.28		
IDP to SRD			
β_9	.09[f]	.06[d]	.06
	.54	.38	.39
β_{11}	.09[f]	.06[d]	.07
	.50	.35	.35
R^2 (η_2) IDP, Wave 2	.11	.28	.26
R^2 (η_5) SRD, Wave 2	.53	.54	.55
R^2 (η_3) IDP, Wave 3	.13	.30	.32
R^2 (η_6) SRD, Wave 3	.54	.56	.55
χ^2 (df)	167.0 (8)	168.3 (10)	163.3 (6)

SOURCE: National Youth Surveys 1976, 1977, 1978.
NOTE: Entries are unstandardized maximum likelihood estimates; standardized coefficients underscored. All coefficients statistically significant at .05 level except those starred.
a, b, c, d, e, f. Coefficients constrained to be equal.

the estimated coefficients. Further modifications to the model, however, should be made because the fit to the data of all three of these models is poor.

The estimation of these models has illustrated the means of identifying complex multiwave systems of equations through imposition of consistency constraints on model parameters, as well as the flexibility of the LISREL or related procedures in estimating a variety of causal effects models. The constraints on parameters in the three-wave approach are likely to be more reasonable than constraints involving the effects of outside exogenous variables, especially when instrumental variables have not been built into the research design.

One final caution concerning the panel models considered in this chapter is that the parameter estimates obtained should indicate that the causal system is "stable" in the sense described in Chapter 2, that is, that it approaches equilibrium at some future time period. As noted earlier, some models may indicate that the system will equilibrate at some point or will "explode," with some or all variances or covariances expanding without limit. Although unstable systems are not technically impossible, obtaining parameter estimates that do not lead the system eventually to equilibrate are usually considered an indication of specification error in the model (Arminger, 1987). For example, consider a simple nonrecursive model where Y_t and X_t are reciprocally related, β_{YX} is the effect from X to Y, β_{XY} is the effect from Y to X, U_Y is the error term for Y, and U_X is the error term for X. In such a model, each variable has an indirect effect on itself, so changes in Y feed back on Y through Y's effect on X and X's effect on Y. This can be seen by substituting the equation for X into the equation for Y:

$$Y_t = \beta_{YX}\beta_{XY}Y_t + \beta_{YX}U_X + U_Y. \tag{3.9}$$

If $\beta_{YX}\beta_{XY}$ is greater than 1, increases in Y will set in motion a process whereby the variance of Y will increase without bound. The system will only stabilize or equilibrate in this model if $\beta_{YX}\beta_{XY}$ is less than 1, and parameter estimates that show otherwise would be inherently suspect. The determination of whether a system will equilibrate becomes difficult to calculate in more complex models and involves manipulation of the **B** matrix of effects between endogenous variables. LISREL conducts this test as the "Stability Index"; the system will equilibrate if its value is less than 1.[10]

4. MEASUREMENT ERROR MODELS

The panel models presented thus far have assumed that the variables in the analyses have been measured without error. As has been well-documented, however, most concepts of interest to social scientists are measured imperfectly with available instruments, such as attitude surveys or published aggregate statistics. To the extent that observed variables contain measurement error, estimates of structural coefficients in regression models will be erroneous and the researcher may make incorrect causal inferences as a result. The problem of measurement error is particularly serious in panel models, as measurement error can lead to the appearance of change in variables over time when no true change took place. However, the repeated measurement of the same variables in panel designs provides useful information for inferring the amount of error in observed items and for estimating the causal effects of independent variables purged of the contaminating effects of imperfect measurement.

Panel data, however, are no cure-all for the problem of measurement error. All of the models that will be considered are valid to the extent that their assumptions can be justified and, in many instances, these assumptions are highly restrictive. They can be relaxed only as the number of indicators and the number of waves of observation increase and, under some conditions, the assumptions themselves may be tested in LISREL or related methods using the equality constraints examined in the previous chapter.

Basic Concepts

Previous monographs in this series have examined the general issue of measurement error in variables and its consequences in some detail (Berry & Feldman, 1985; Carmines & Zeller, 1979; Markus, 1979; Sullivan & Feldman, 1979). Instead of measuring the concept of interest perfectly, most indicators used in empirical analyses contain some amount of error. This error is either *systematic*, in which case the measuring instrument may be viewed as tapping other factors aside from the theoretical variable of interest, or *random*, in which case the indicator is measuring the true concept plus some "noise" component. In survey data, for example, random noise may be present because of ambiguous questions, restricted response categories, guessing, or other random factors that influence the verbal response of the interviewee at a given point in time. As systematic error increases, the *validity* of the indicator decreases, whereas increases in random error are associated with decreases in the indicator's *reliability*.

The models discussed here will focus on correcting for random error in empirical indicators; for more detailed methods for detecting and handling systematic error, see Carmines and Zeller (1979).

The basic random measurement error model for y_{kt}, the kth indicator of the true-score, or "latent variable" η_t at time t may be expressed as

$$y_{kt} = \lambda_{kt} \eta_t + \epsilon_{kt} \tag{4.1}$$

where λ_{kt} is an unstandardized coefficient linking y_{kt} with the latent variable η_t, and ϵ_{kt} is a random disturbance term. We use LISREL notation for the variables and measurement parameters to facilitate the use of these procedures for estimating the models in this chapter. In single-indicator measurement models, λ_{kt} is set to 1 so that the scale of the indicator and the latent variable are identical; in multiple-indicator models, the scale of the latent variable must be set by fixing one of the λ_{kt} to equal 1.[11] The usual assumptions about ϵ_{kt} are that it has a mean of zero, constant variance at all levels of η_t, and is also uncorrelated with the structural disturbance term for η_t. Under these conditions for the single-indicator case, $\sigma^2_{y_{kt}}$, the variance of the observed indicator y_{kt}, is equal to

$$\sigma^2_{y_{kt}} = \sigma^2_{\eta_t} + \sigma^2_{\epsilon_{kt}} \tag{4.2}$$

where $\sigma^2_{\eta_t}$ is the variance of the latent variable η_t, and $\sigma^2_{\epsilon_{kt}}$ is the variance of ϵ_{kt}, the random error component in y_{kt}. Thus the variance of the observed indicator is composed of two parts: "true-score" variance, represented by the variance of the latent variable η_t, and random error variance. The *reliability* ρ_{yy} of an observed indicator is simply the proportion of the indicator's variance that is "true-score" variance, or

$$\rho_{yy} = \frac{\sigma^2_{\eta_t}}{\sigma^2_{\eta_t} + \sigma^2_{\epsilon_{kt}}}. \tag{4.3}$$

In other words, reliability is the ratio of true-score variance to observed variance in an indicator; the closer the value is to 1, the less random error is contained in an indicator of a latent concept.

Whenever the λ_{kt} are not set to 1, as in multiple-indicator and standardized measurement models, then the reliability of an indicator is

$$\rho_{yy} = \frac{\lambda_{kt}^2 \sigma_{\eta_t}^2}{\lambda_{kt}^2 \sigma_{\eta_t}^2 + \sigma_{\epsilon_{kt}}^2} \qquad (4.4)$$

(Wheaton, Muthen, Alwin, & Summers, 1977, p. 108).

When an indicator with random measurement error is used as an independent variable in a regression equation, the result is biased estimation of the true causal effect of the latent variable, because it can be shown that the independent variable is no longer unrelated to the disturbance term in the estimation equation (Markus, 1979, p. 55).[12] In a bivariate regression model, the estimated coefficient will be equal to the true coefficient multiplied by the reliability of the indicator; thus unreliable measures will lead to underestimation, or attenuation, of a variable's effects. In multivariate models, however, the direction of the bias may be in either direction, and the presence of measurement error in any one of the independent variables may lead to substantial bias in estimating the effects of all other variables in the model as well, even those that are presumed to be measured without error.

The problem of measurement error in some ways is even more acute in the panel context. As has been shown throughout the monograph, most panel models are variants of the conditional change or static-score model in which Y_t is a function of Y_{t-1} and some set of independent variables X_t, X_{t-1}, and so on. We noted in Chapter 2 that the lagged endogenous variable Y_{t-1} serves several purposes in these models: as a control for "regression to the mean" and "negative feedback" as systems move toward equilibrium, as a proxy for omitted causal paths, and as a substantive variable affecting Y_t in its own right. Omitting Y_{t-1} typically results in bias in parameter estimates because of the likely *negative* correlation between Y_{t-1} and ΔY; but given measurement error in Y_{t-1} of the form in Equation (4.1), where $\lambda_{kt} = 1$ and the ϵ_{kt} are uncorrelated with the η_t true-scores and with each other over time, it can be shown that

$$\text{Cov}(Y_{t-1}, \Delta Y) = \text{Cov}(\eta_{t-1}, \Delta \eta) - \text{Var}(\epsilon_{t-1}) \qquad (4.5)$$

whenever the error variances are equal over time. That is, the covariance of the observed Y_{t-1} and subsequent change is equal to the covariance of the "true-score" at time $t-1$ and the "true subsequent change" minus the variance of the measurement errors in Y_{t-1}. The implication of this equation is that unless measurement errors in Y_{t-1} are controlled, the conditional-change models analyzed thus far will lead to a larger negative estimate of the covariation between Y_{t-1} and subsequent change, and an underestimation of the effect of Y_{t-1} on Y_t relative to the effect of the "true-score" η_{t-1} on η_t. This in turn will often lead to an overestimation of the causal effects of other variables on Y_t to the extent that they are positively related to the observed Y_{t-1}. On the other hand, if the measurement errors in Y are correlated with one another over time, this may lead to an overestimation of the effect of Y_{t-1} on Y_t, and a corresponding underestimation of the effects of other variables if these errors are not taken into account. Consequently, measurement error in the lagged endogenous variable is one of the most serious obstacles to successful causal inference in the panel context, and it is essential to build models that take measurement error into account when estimating structural effects.

Although measurement error leads to serious problems in panel analysis, it can also be handled much more easily than in the cross-sectional context. With cross-sectional data, two procedures commonly are used for handling the problem of measurement error. One is the instrumental variables approach, or Two Stage Least Squares estimation, similar to the procedures discussed for the structural models from the previous chapter. Because the biases in the OLS estimates in the presence of measurement error are caused by the correlation between the independent variable and the disturbance term in the equation, a possible solution is to include in the model an exogenous variable (that is by definition uncorrelated with the structural disturbance) that is related to the true-score or latent variable but unrelated to its random error term (Berry & Feldman, 1985, pp. 34-37).

With panel data, alternative strategies for handling the problem of measurement error are available, and in most cases will be preferred over the instrumental variables or Two Stage Least Squares procedure. Because of the difficulty in finding suitable instruments, especially in secondary analyses, the two stage approach depends on assumptions about the independence of the instrumental variable and the disturbance term that may not hold in a given model, and the low correlation between the error-laden independent variable and its instrument often results in very imprecise estimates in the second stage. Also, although the instrumental variable technique under ideal conditions can provide consistent estimates of the structural parameters linking the latent variables in a model, it provides no direct information about the reliability, error variance, or other measurement properties of indicators, which often is an important goal of empirical research. Thus the instrumental variable procedure poses some potential drawbacks for the panel analyst.

The other procedure developed for dealing with measurement error is the multiple-indicators approach, in which several measures of the same latent variable are employed to generate estimates of both the structural effects and measurement parameters in a particular model (Sullivan & Feldman, 1979). In panel designs, the repeated measurement of the indicators over time increases the power of this approach considerably, as additional waves of data provide more information with which to estimate relevant structural and measurement coefficients. In fact, measurement properties and structural effects in models with only one indicator of a latent variable can be estimated with at least three waves of data, and thus all multiwave panel models can be treated as variants of the multiple-indicators approach. The full power of the procedures, however, will be seen in models with multiple indicators and multiple waves of measurement and, in some cases, it will be possible to estimate models that include correlated errors of measurement and correlated structural disturbances terms across time. These analyses will provide the most complete information regarding each item's reliability, the stability of the latent variables, and the structural effects linking the latent variables together in a causal model.

Single-Indicator Models

Two-Wave Models

When only two waves of data are available, the options for handling measurement error in a single indicator y_t are limited. Following LISREL-type notation for convenience, if y_t is the observed indicator of the latent variable η_t at time t, ϵ_t is the error variance in y at time t, β_1 is the stability coefficient linking the latent variable from time $t-1$ to time t, γ_k are effects of the exogenous variables ξ on η_t, and ζ_t is the structural disturbance of the latent variable, we may express the structural model of interest as

$$\eta_t = \beta_1 \eta_{t-1} + \sum \gamma_k \xi_k + \zeta_t . \tag{4.6}$$

But using the imperfectly measured observed variables y_{t-1} and y_t means that the estimation model contains the true-score η as well as measurement error:

$$(\eta_t + \epsilon_t) = \beta_1(\eta_{t-1} + \epsilon_{t-1}) + \sum \gamma_k \xi_k + \zeta_t . \tag{4.7}$$

From this equation, it is clear that the model is not identified, as there is no way to separate the true-score and error portions of the observed variables even if one assumes that the variances of the measurement errors for the two indicators are equal.

McAdams (1986) outlines several alternatives for estimating this model in LISREL by imposing additional restrictions on the parameters in the equation. The analyst might constrain the value of β_1 to be equal to 1, in which case the model reduces to a variant of the unconditional change-score model discussed in Chapter 2, with Δy being predicted by a series of X variables. Another possibility is to constrain the value of ζ_t, which fixes the total explained variance in the equation. Finally, ϵ_t can be constrained to fix the reliability of y_t to some known or assumed value.

These procedures can be used as exploratory devices with two-wave data to produce a series of estimates of the parameters in Equation (4.7), and the analyst can evaluate the results to obtain the depiction of the underlying causal process that emerges from different restrictions on the model, or to obtain estimates of the range of possible values of the equation's parameters. But the restrictions that are necessary to identify the model are problematic. Constraining β_1 to be 1 ignores any negative effect from y_t on Δy that does not arise from measurement error, and constraining the variance of ζ_t or the ϵ_t is usually not viable because likely values of the equation's overall error variance or the amount of error variance of the observed indicators are usually not known in advance. Obviously, we would like to estimate the values of β_1 and the variances of the ζ_t and ϵ_t without these constraints, and for this more waves of information are necessary.

Three-Wave Models

Models for the analysis of a single indicator of a latent variable have been developed for three-wave data by Wiley and Wiley (1970) and Heise (1969). The general three-wave model is shown in diagram form in Figure 4.1.

The set of *measurement* equations linking the indicators to their latent variables may be written as follows:

$$y_1 = \lambda_{11}\eta_1 + \epsilon_1$$

$$y_2 = \lambda_{22}\eta_2 + \epsilon_2 \qquad (4.8)$$

$$y_3 = \lambda_{33}\eta_3 + \epsilon_3$$

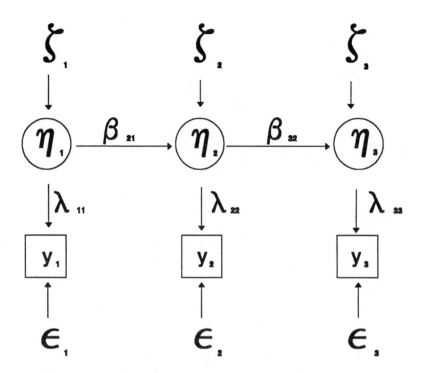

Figure 4.1. Three-Wave Single-Indicator Measurement Model

where the λ_{tt} are coefficients linking each indicator y to its corresponding latent variable η. The set of *structural* equations describing the causal linkages between the latent (endogenous) variables is

$$\eta_1 = \zeta_1$$

$$\eta_2 = \beta_{21}\eta_1 + \zeta_2 \qquad (4.9)$$

$$\eta_3 = \beta_{32}\eta_2 + \zeta_3 .$$

The standard set of assumptions for the measurement errors and the structural disturbances are that the covariances between the ϵ_t and the η_t and between the ϵ_t and the ζ_t are all zero. Further, the measurement errors are assumed to be randomly distributed with a mean of zero, constant variance, and uncorrelated with one another over time. The ζ_t disturbance terms are also assumed to be random, with mean zero, constant variance, and uncorrelated over time.

At this point, the model's parameters are not identified. Because there are 11 "unknowns," or free parameters (3 ϵ_t, 3 λ_{tt}, 3 variances of the ζ_t, and 2 β coefficients) and only 6 "knowns," the variances and covariances of the observed indicators, there is not enough information available to obtain unique estimates of the parameters' values. Hence additional assumptions must be made that place certain constraints on the model's parameters.

In the Heise procedure, the model is identified by standardizing both the latent variables and observed indicators and by constraining the reliability of the indicator y to be equal in all three time periods. By standardizing the model, the variances of the η_t are 1, which means that the only free parameters in the structural portion of the model are the stability coefficients β_{21} and β_{32}. Because the observed indicators are also standardized, the only free parameters in the measurement portion of the model are the λ_{tt}, as the variances of the ϵ_t are necessarily equal to $1 - \lambda_{tt}^2$.[13] It follows that the reliabilities of the indicators, according to Equation (4.4), are simply λ_{tt}^2, because the variance of the η_t and the denominator in Equation (4.4) are both equal to 1. Setting the reliabilities to be equal across waves, then, implies that the λ_{tt} are equal, resulting in a just-identified model with three free parameters and three correlations between the observed indicators with which to estimate them. It is straightforward to solve for the three parameters in terms of the observed correlations:

$$\lambda = \sqrt{\frac{r_{12}\, r_{23}}{r_{13}}}$$

$$\beta_{21} = \frac{r_{13}}{r_{23}} \qquad (4.10)$$

$$\beta_{32} = \frac{r_{13}}{r_{12}}$$

The reliability of y is simply the square of the first expression in Equation (4.10), because λ^2 is equal to the variance in y "explained" by the latent variable η_t.

The Wiley and Wiley procedure achieves identification in an *unstandardized* model by constraining the error variances of the indicator to be equal over time, that is, $\sigma^2_{\epsilon_1} = \sigma^2_{\epsilon_2} = \sigma^2_{\epsilon_3}$, gaining 2 degrees of freedom in the process. In an unstandardized model, because the variance in η_t is no longer constrained to be 1, the indeterminacy in the scale of the unobserved η_t variables is solved by setting each of the λ_{tt} to equal 1. Given these constraints, parameter estimates can be obtained through algebraic manipulation of the variances and covariances of the observed variables in the following fashion. Substituting the structural equation predictions from Equation (4.9) for the three latent variables into the measurement equations from Equation (4.8) yields the following:

$$y_1 = \zeta_1 + \epsilon$$

$$y_2 = \beta_{21}\zeta_1 + \zeta_2 + \epsilon \qquad (4.11)$$

$$y_3 = \beta_{32}(\beta_{21}\zeta_1 + \zeta_2) + \zeta_3 + \epsilon .$$

Taking expected values of the variances and covariances of these y results in

$$\text{Var}(y_1) = \text{Var}(\zeta_1) + \text{Var}(\epsilon)$$

$$\text{Cov}(y_1 y_2) = \beta_{21} \text{Var}(\zeta_1)$$

$$\text{Cov}(y_1 y_3) = \beta_{21}\beta_{32} \text{Var}(\zeta_1)$$

$$\text{Var}(y_2) = \beta_{21}^2 \text{Var}(\zeta_1) + \text{Var}(\zeta_2) + \text{Var}(\epsilon) \qquad (4.12)$$

$$\text{Cov}(y_2 y_3) = \beta_{32}\left[\beta_{21}^2 \text{Var}(\zeta_1) + \text{Var}(\zeta_2) \right]$$

$$\text{Var}(y_3) = \beta_{32}^2\left[\beta_{21}^2 \text{Var}(\zeta_1) + \text{Var}(\zeta_2) \right] + \text{Var}(\zeta_3) + \text{Var}(\epsilon) .$$

It can be seen that the model is just-identified, with 6 free parameters (the variances of the three ζ_t, β_{21}, β_{32}, and the variance of ϵ) and 6 observed variances and covariances with which to estimate them. Solving for the variance of ϵ and the two stability coefficients yields

$$\text{Var}(\epsilon) = \text{Var}(y_2) - \frac{\text{Cov}(y_2 y_3)\text{Cov}(y_1 y_2)}{\text{Cov}(y_1 y_3)}$$

$$\beta_{21} = \frac{\text{Cov}(y_1 y_2)}{\text{Var}(y_1) - \text{Var}(\epsilon)} \qquad (4.13)$$

$$\beta_{32} = \frac{\text{Cov}(y_1 y_3)}{\text{Cov}(y_1 y_2)} .$$

Once these estimates are obtained, it is straightforward to calculate the reliabilities of each indicator according to Equation (4.3). Because in this just-identified model, $\text{Var}(\eta_t) = \text{Var}(y_t) - \text{Var}(\epsilon)$ exactly, then the reliability of each indicator is simply $[\text{Var}(y_t) - \text{Var}(\epsilon)]/\text{Var}(y_t)$.

Combining Single-Indicator and Structural Models in LISREL

The coefficients for the models considered thus far may also be obtained through maximum likelihood methods in LISREL. Although in this just-identified case the parameter estimates will be identical to those described above, LISREL will also provide the maximum likelihood standard errors, which are otherwise difficult to estimate. These procedures easily can be extended to estimate parameters in four-wave and longer single-indicator models, and in models with multiple indicators of latent variables. LISREL may also be used to model measurement error in variables in the context of more complex structural models of the form described in the previous two chapters, and, if such models are overidentified, LISREL provides efficient estimates of all parameters as well as tests of the model's goodness of fit.

We illustrate these procedures by estimating measurement and structural parameters for the party identification and candidate evaluation models of Chapter 3. The results are presented in Table 4.1.

Column (1) in the table contains the results of separate Wiley-Wiley estimation of measurement error and true-score stability in the party identification and candidate ratings variables over time. In setting up these models in LISREL, the coefficients linking the latent η_t variables are the off-diagonal elements of the **B** matrix, the coefficients representing the structural disturbances are the diagonal elements of the **Ψ** matrix, the

TABLE 4.1
Three-Wave Models With Measurement Error

	Model	
	(1)	(2)
Error Variances		
θ_ϵ, Party Identification	.55	.55
θ_ϵ, Candidate Evaluations	225.7	225.8
Stabilities		
$PID_1 - PID_2$	1.02	1.01[a]
	.98	.98
$PID_2 - PID_3$	1.01	1.01[a]
	1.00	1.01
$THERM_1 - THERM_2$	.98	.85[b]
	.87	.78
$THERM_2 - THERM_3$	.90	.85[b]
	.84	.79
Cross-Lagged Effects		
$PID_1 - THERM_2$	——	2.82[c]
		.15
$PID_2 - THERM_3$	——	2.82[c]
		.15
$THERM_1 - PID_2$	——	.001[d]***
		.01
$THERM_2 - PID_3$	——	.001[d]***
		.01
Reliabilities		
PID_1	.86	.86
PID_2	.87	.87
PID_3	.87	.87
$THERM_1$	.81	.81
$THERM_2$	.84	.84
$THERM_3$	.85	.85
χ^2 (df)	0.0 (0)	12.7 (7)

SOURCE: American National Election Study, Major Panel File, 1980.
NOTE: Entries are maximum likelihood estimates; standardized coefficients underscored. All coefficients statistically significant except those starred.
N for all models is 733.
a, b, c, d. Coefficients constrained to be equal.

coefficients representing the λ_y linking the latent variables to their observed indicators are the main diagonal elements in Λ_y, and the measurement error variances are the main diagonal elements of Θ_ϵ. The λ_y are set equal to 1 and the θ_ϵ are constrained to be equal across waves. The estimate of error variance in the party identification scale is .55, and the true-score standardized stabilities of party identification are .98 from wave 1 to wave 2 and 1.0 from wave 2 to wave 3. In contrast to the observed wave 1-wave 2 correlation of .87 and the observed wave 2-wave 3 correlation of .88, these estimates indicate that the true-score stability after correcting for measurement error in the indicators is nearly perfect. The reliabilities of the scale may be computed from the formula given in Equation (4.3) as .86 in the first wave, .87 in the second wave, and .87 in the third. The corresponding results for the candidate ratings variable show an estimated error variance of 225.5, corrected stability estimates of .88 and .89, and estimated reliabilities of .81 in the first wave, .84 in the second wave, and .85 in the third.

These methods may be used in models that also contain structural effects between variables in several ways. One method is to fix the error variances of the indicators to equal the values obtained in the initial Wiley-Wiley runs, and the estimation of structural effects can proceed by adding this information to any of the models estimated in the previous two chapters. Alternatively, LISREL will produce simultaneously the estimates of measurement error and structural coefficients, provided all parameters are identified. As an example of this procedure, Column (2) in the table shows the results of reestimating the full three-wave cross-lagged reciprocal effects model from Chapter 3. The model shows a significant effect only from party identification to candidate ratings, in contrast to the reciprocal effects estimated in earlier models that assumed no measurement error. The estimates of error variance for both party identification and candidate evaluation are statistically significant. Moreover, the fit of this model to the data is excellent, with a χ^2 value of 12.5 with 7 degrees of freedom, indicating that the model cannot be rejected as holding in the population ($p > .05$). These models demonstrate that causal effects found in panel models may be quite different once measurement error is taken into account, leading the analyst to different conclusions regarding the substantive relationship between variables.

Four-Wave and Longer Single-Indicator Models

The Wiley-Wiley and Heise models are useful for estimating measurement properties of indicators and structural coefficients with three-wave panel data. However, the assumptions and constraints contained in these models may at times be difficult to justify. In particular, the assumption of equal reliabilities in the Heise model or equal error variances in the Wiley and Wiley model are especially problematic because there is no a priori reason to suspect that either the variances of the latent variables (which figure in calculations of reliability) or the variances of the errors will be constant over time.[14] In fact, Jagodzinski, Kühnel, and Schmidt (1987) show that in many instances, the error variance of indicators decreases over time, which accounts in their view for why "the models proposed by Wiley and Wiley . . . and Heise . . . frequently fail in short-wave panel studies" (pp. 294-295).

Further, because the models are just-identified (if no other endogenous or exogenous variables are included), there is no way to test the fit of the model as a whole, because each will account for the observed data perfectly. In some instances, implausible empirical results, such as estimates of negative error variance in the Wiley and Wiley approach, or estimates of reliabilities or standardized stability coefficients that are substantially greater than 1 in either procedure, will provide an indication that the model is inapplicable. But there is no way to determine whether the measurement model or the structural model is misspecified.

Finally, the assumption of uncorrelated measurement error is also problematic because identical items may contain some common variance over time apart from their relation to the latent variable. Correlated measurement errors in survey designs may arise from memory effects, similar wordings, or meanings of items that induce similar responses over time, independent of causes stemming from the latent variable of which the item is an indicator. The practical consequence of omitting the error correlations is a probable inflation of the estimate of the true-score stability, as the stability in the true-scores induced by the correlated errors of measurement is absorbed into the estimates of the β parameters.

The estimation and evaluation of single-indicator measurement models is eased somewhat with the addition of more waves of information (see Feldman, 1989, and Green & Palmquist, 1990, for applications). The first advantage is that some of the parameters in the longer-wave models may be overidentified. In those cases, the fit of the model as a whole can be tested either by computing separate estimates of overidentified parameters algebraically and comparing their values or by using LISREL to obtain the maximum likelihood estimates of the parameters and using the χ^2 goodness-of-fit test to evaluate the extent to which the model accounts for the variances and covariances of the observed indicators. Werts, Jöreskog, and

Linn (1971) extend the Wiley-Wiley model in Figure 4.1 to four waves and show that the error variances and true-score variances (and hence the reliabilities) of the "inner" indicators y_2 and y_3 are identified, and that the estimate of the stability of the latent variable from time 2 to time 3, β_{32}, is overidentified. In terms of the observed correlations, $\beta_{32} = r_{13} r_{24} / r_{12} r_{34}$ and $\beta_{32} = r_{14} r_{23} / r_{12} r_{34}$. With longer-wave panels, more parameters will be overidentified.

A second advantage of longer-wave panels is that the additional information allows more efficient testing of models with correlated errors and an increased ability to compare such models to models with random error. Correlated measurement error models have been proposed for three-wave panels by Wiley and Wiley (1974), but estimation of such just-identified models has often yielded anomalous results such as negative error variances and covariances and implausible stability estimates. With four-wave data, a model that assumes equal stability of the η, equal error variances, and equal error covariances is overidentified with 3 degrees of freedom (10 observed variances and covariances minus 7 free parameters—4 ψ variances of the disturbances, 1 β, 1 error variance, and 1 error covariance). Palmquist and Green (1989), however, show that the estimates from this model are relatively inefficient under conditions of low indicator reliability and low true-score stability. Moreover, they note that as the number of waves of information increases, the plausibility of the equal stability and equal error variances and covariances may decline significantly. But four waves of information provide the distinct advantage that alternative models can be assessed through χ^2 goodness-of-fit measures as well as through examination of the plausibility of the parameter estimates.

Multiple-Indicator Models

When more than one indicator of a latent variable is available, many of the limitations of single-indicator measurement models can be overcome. If two indicators are present, some restrictive models may be estimated with only two waves of measurement. As more indicators and more waves are available, overidentified models that incorporate correlated measurement errors over time can be estimated and tested with global goodness-of-fit statistics. The researcher may also impose a variety of constraints on the parameters in the models and test these restrictions by relaxing them and comparing the summary χ^2 measures of alternative models. In these

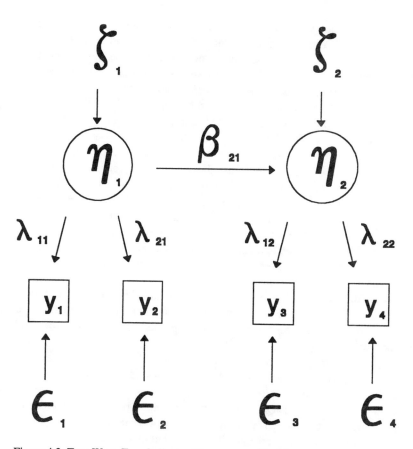

Figure 4.2. Two-Wave Two-Indicator Measurement Model

ways, the multiple-indicators approach provides far more flexibility and power in estimating and evaluating measurement models.

The Two-Wave Two-Indicator Model

The simplest extension of the models discussed thus far is the addition of one other indicator, y_{2t}, of the latent variable η_t. This addition enables the measurement model shown in Figure 4.2 to be estimated with only two waves of data.

In this model, y_1 and y_3 are one indicator of the latent variable η at time 1 and time 2 respectively, and y_2 and y_4 are the second indicator of η at each panel wave. The lagged latent variable is specified to have an effect on its value at the second wave. We make the following initial assumptions in this model: (a) all variables, error terms, and structural disturbances are expressed in mean deviation form; (b) the error terms ϵ_t and ζ_t are normally distributed; (c) the ϵ_t are uncorrelated with the η_t and the ζ_t; (d) η_1 and ζ_2 are uncorrelated; (e) the ζ_t are uncorrelated across time; and (f) the measurement error terms are uncorrelated with one another. The scale of the latent variables is set by fixing the λ coefficient for y_1 and y_3 to be 1 (although this could have been done for y_2 and y_4 instead).

The model has 9 free parameters to be estimated (the variances of ζ_1 and ζ_2, β_{21}, λ_{21}, and λ_{22}, and the four error variances), and the 10 observed variances and covariances among the observed indicators result in 1 degree of freedom with which to test the model. Once the estimates are obtained through LISREL or related methods, the reliability of each indicator may be calculated as in Equation (4.4) above.

In addition to needing only two waves of data for estimation, this model has several appealing features. First, the researcher may constrain the λ and θ_ϵ in various ways to test the measurement properties of the indicators, and each restriction yields degrees of freedom necessary to test its applicability. In the psychometric literature, y_1 and y_2 are described as *parallel* measures of η_1 if $\lambda_{11} = \lambda_{21}$, and $\theta_{\epsilon_1} = \theta_{\epsilon_2}$. This may be tested in LISREL by setting both lambda coefficients to be 1 and equating the two error variances within each point in time. These restrictions for both waves add 4 degrees of freedom with which to test their applicability. Alternatively, y_1 and y_2 may be *tau-equivalent* measures of η_1 if $\lambda_{11} = \lambda_{21}$ but their error variances differ from one another. This may be tested simply by setting both lambda coefficients to be 1, and the resultant gain is 2 degrees of freedom. In the model of Figure 4.2, the measures are termed *congeneric*; the coefficients linking the indicators to the latent variable differ, as do the indicators' error variances.

Further restrictions may be imposed by equating the error variances of the same indicator at different points in time (e.g., $\theta_{\epsilon_1} = \theta_{\epsilon_3}$) or equating the lambda coefficients for the same indicator over time as well (e.g., $\lambda_{11} = \lambda_{12}$). Each of these constraints may be tested in terms of relative model fit. The latter restriction of equal λ for the same indicator across all time periods is especially important in panel models and amounts to an assumption that an unobserved latent variable has the same unstandardized effect on a given indicator in each panel wave. Wheaton et al. (1977, p. 129) claim that this assumption is an essential element of any model that "purports to interpret a [latent] variable's stability: it . . . means that we are expected to measure the same construct [over time]. Strictly speaking, the concept of stability *demands* this specification" (emphasis added). Thus there will generally be a presumption to constrain the λ to be equal over time, and these constraints may be tested in LISREL or related procedures against an unconstrained model through the χ^2 difference test.

The main limitation of the two-indicator, two-wave model is that it specifies no correlated errors between identical items measured at different points in time. Costner (1969) and Sullivan and Feldman (1979) note that the only parameter that is overidentified in the model of Figure 4.2 is the stability coefficient β_{21}, for which there are two estimates. Hence the assessment of model fit, either through the LISREL χ^2 or by computing the two estimates and comparing their values, provides a test of the possible existence of correlated measurement errors over time, because the estimated true-score stability in the model would then (if the correlated errors are positive) not be sufficient to explain the observed correlations between indicators at different waves. Unfortunately, if correlated measurement errors are included, the model in Figure 4.2 is underidentified. In order to estimate those parameters, three options are available: (a) in two-wave models, include more indicators of the latent variable; (b) add at least one exogenous "background" variable into the two-wave model that affects the latent variable at both points in time; or (c) add additional waves of information. All of these strategies will identify the model without imposing any constraints on the measurement error matrices. The first and third options are preferred because the resultant models will have enough degrees of freedom to impose and relax various constraints on the parameter estimates. The second strategy will be necessary when neither additional indicators nor waves of information are available.

A Two-Wave Example With Three Indicators

The model shown in Figure 4.3 displays a two-wave model with three indicators of legal political protest potential from the West German protest data described in previous chapters. Note that correlated errors between the same indicators over time are represented by the free error covariances between identical indicators at the two points in time, that is, $\theta_{\epsilon_{41}}$, $\theta_{\epsilon_{52}}$, $\theta_{\epsilon_{63}}$. y_1 and y_4 are responses in waves 1 and 2 to potential for participating

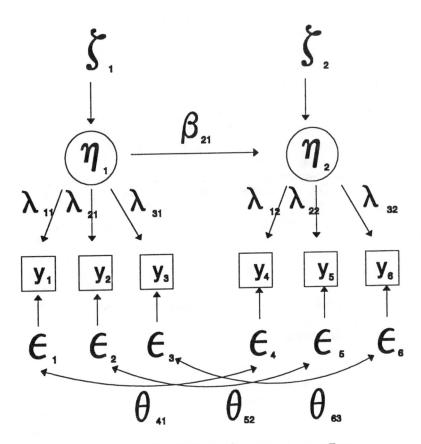

Figure 4.3. Three-Indicator Model With Correlated Measurement Errors

in "a permitted demonstration," y_2 and y_5 potential for "working with a citizen's action group," and y_3 and y_6 potential for "collecting signatures for a petition."

There are $(6 \times 7)/2$, or 21, observed variances and covariances in the model, and 16 free parameters—the variances of ζ_1 and ζ_2, β_{21}, λ_{21}, λ_{31}, λ_{22}, λ_{32}, 6 error variances of the observed indicators, and 3 covariances between the errors for each indicator over time. The scale of the latent variable is set by fixing λ_{11} and λ_{12} at 1. There are 5 degrees of freedom in the model. Table 4.2 shows the LISREL maximum likelihood estimates for several variants of this model.

TABLE 4.2
Two-Wave Three-Indicator Models
With and Without Correlated Measurement Errors

	Correlated Error Model (1)	No Correlated Error Model (2)
Measurement Coefficients		
λ_{11}	1.00[a]	1.00[a]
	.68	.70
λ_{21}	1.12*	1.11*
	.68	.69
λ_{31}	1.59*	1.48*
	.91	.88
λ_{12}	1.00[a]	1.00[a]
	.75	.79
λ_{22}	1.11*	1.06*
	.77	.79
λ_{32}	1.41*	1.30*
	.91	.89
θ_{11}	3.92*	3.66*
θ_{22}	4.85*	4.66*
θ_{33}	1.69*	2.36*
θ_{44}	3.34*	3.11*
θ_{55}	3.68*	3.42*
θ_{66}	1.80*	2.28*
θ_{41}	1.47*	——
θ_{52}	.91*	——
θ_{63}	−.74*	——
Stability Coefficients		
β_{21}	.62*	.64*
	.54	.54
$R^2 (\eta_2)$	.29	.29
χ^2 (df)	12.5 (5)	69.8 (8)

NOTE: Entries are unstandardized maximum likelihood estimates. Standardized coefficients underscored. N for all models is 377.
a. Coefficient fixed at 1.
* Significant at .05 level.

The results shown in the first column of the table correspond to the correlated error model in Figure 4.3. As can be seen, all parameter estimates are statistically significant, including all covariances between the measurement errors of each indicator over time (θ_{41}, θ_{52}, θ_{63}). The estimated covariance between the "signing petition" indicators (y_3 and y_6) is negative, an implausible result that will be discussed in the context of negative autocorrelation in Chapter 5. The reliabilities of the indicators may be obtained by squaring the standardized λ_y coefficients, because in the fully standardized model the variances of both η and y are 1.[15] In this case, the reliabilities are in the .5 to .8 range, indicating that a substantial amount of random measurement error is present in the observed variables. The unstandardized stability of the latent "legal protest potential" variable is estimated to be .62, with a standardized effect of .54. The goodness of fit for the model, as measured by χ^2, is 12.5 with 5 degrees of freedom, indicating a relatively good fit of the model to the observed data.

In the second column, a model is estimated *without* the free error covariances, and the resultant fit is much worse, with a χ^2 value of 69.8 with 8 degrees of freedom. Because this model is identical to the model in Column (1) except for the constraint that $\theta_{\epsilon_{41}} = \theta_{\epsilon_{52}} = \theta_{\epsilon_{63}} = 0$, the improvement in fit that results from relaxing the constraint can be tested by comparing the two χ^2 values. In this case, the difference is 57.3 with 3 degrees of freedom, and the improvement in fit brought about by allowing covariances between the error terms is statistically significant. Substantively, however, the error covariances are not large because the difference in the unstandardized stability between the two models is very low, and there is no difference between the two standardized stability estimates.

Several alternative measurement models may also be tested within the LISREL framework. One recommended model constrains the λ coefficients for each indicator to be equal in waves 1 and 2 in accordance with Wheaton et al.'s (1977) assertion that this ensures the similarity of the latent variables over time. The model gains 2 degrees of freedom by imposing this constraint, and in this instance the χ^2 difference is 2.7, which is not statistically significant at the .05 level. Thus it may be concluded that the equality constraint is satisfied with these data. Other models could constrain the error variances for similar indicators to be equal over time, or could free the covariances of the errors for different indicators at the same point in time if there were theoretical reasons to suspect some common variation between indicators that was unrelated to the latent variable. It is also possible to compare the measurement coefficients and stabilities of the latent variables for different subgroups in the population.

The reader is referred to the discussion of group differences in Jöreskog and Sörbom (1989, Chapter 9) and applications of the procedures may be found in Judd, Krosnick, and Milburn (1981) and Porst, Schmidt, and Zeifang (1987).

Combining Multiple-Indicator and Structural Models

Measurement models of this type can be incorporated into more complex causal systems in a straightforward manner. Models can be specified that assume that the latent variables η_1 and η_2 in Figure 4.3 are influenced by a set of exogenous variables or other endogenous variables, with the additional variables being measured with or without an error component. In LISREL, the $\mathbf{B}$, $\mathbf{\Psi}$, $\mathbf{\Lambda}_y$, $\mathbf{\Theta}_\epsilon$ would be modified to characterize the new system of measurement and structural equations for the endogenous variables and, if exogenous variables are present, additional matrices for their measurement models $(\mathbf{\Lambda}_x, \mathbf{\Theta}_\delta)$ and structural effects $(\mathbf{\Phi}, \mathbf{\Gamma})$ would be specified as well.

For example, we test for cross-lagged and synchronous causal effects between legal protest potential and group memberships in the two-wave German protest data using the three indicators to measure protest potential. We assume that group memberships in waves 1 and 2 are measured without error; with a single indicator at two points in time, plausible measurement models for this variable are not identified. Thus the measurement error matrices in LISREL are revised to reflect two new endogenous variables (GROUPS$_1$ and GROUPS$_2$) that are perfectly measured $(\lambda = 1, \theta_\epsilon = 0)$, structural effects between the GROUPS and PROTEST latent variables are specified in the $\mathbf{B}$ matrix, and structural disturbance variances and covariances of the latent variables are specified in the $\mathbf{\Psi}$ matrix. Recall from the previous chapter that a two-wave model with both cross-lagged and synchronous reciprocal effects is not identified without the addition of outside exogenous variables that influence one of the variables of interest but not the other. Thus to estimate the model an instrumental variable for legal protest potential in wave 2 must be specified, as well as an instrumental variable for group memberships in wave 2. These exogenous ξ variables are specified to have effects on only one of the two reciprocally related wave 2 variables. Such variables were not built into the data collection of this study; however, the survey contains information about the respondent's potential for participation in *illegal* political activities, such as participating in a demonstration that breaks the law, and information about the respondent's self-reported memberships in groups that encourage *ille-*

gal protest behaviors. If we assume that potential for *illegal* protest in 1989 influences PROTEST$_2$ but is uncorrelated with the GROUP$_2$ equation's disturbance, and that 1989 *illegal* group memberships influence GROUPS$_2$ but are uncorrelated with PROTEST$_2$'s disturbance term, then these outside variables may be used as instruments to identify the model. The maximum likelihood estimates from this model for the relationship between GROUPS and PROTEST across the two waves are

$$\text{PROTEST}_2 = \underset{\substack{(.11) \\ \underline{.41}}}{.45 \text{ PROTEST}_1} + \underset{\substack{(.57) \\ \underline{.45}}}{1.13 \text{ GROUPS}_2} + \underset{\substack{(.27) \\ \underline{-.07}}}{-.20 \text{ GROUPS}_1}$$

$$(4.14)$$

$$\text{GROUPS}_2 = \underset{\substack{(.07) \\ \underline{.25}}}{.27 \text{ GROUPS}_1} + \underset{\substack{(.11) \\ \underline{-.03}}}{-.01 \text{ PROTEST}_2} + \underset{\substack{(.06) \\ \underline{.25}}}{.11 \text{ PROTEST}_1} \,.$$

These estimates suggest that the relationship between GROUPS and PROTEST follows the same type of feedback process seen in the analysis of peer involvement and delinquency with the three-wave National Youth Survey data; protest potential has a significant lagged effect on group memberships in wave 2 (controlling for its initial values), and group memberships has a synchronous effect on protest potential.

Identifying Two-Indicator Measurement Models
With Background Variables

In some instances, three indicators are not available for estimating measurement models that include correlated error terms. Under these conditions, it is still possible to identify the two-wave, two-indicator measurement model in Figure 4.2 that includes correlated measurement errors if there is at least one background variable that affects the latent variable at both points in time (Dwyer, 1983, p. 400). The model would be specified in LISREL by including the background variable as an exogenous ξ variable, and its effects specified as free parameters in the Γ matrix. The total number of free parameters, once one of the λ coefficients is set to 1 in each wave, is now 14: the variances of ζ_1 and ζ_2, β_{21}, λ_{21}, λ_{22}, the 4 error variances and 2 error covariances, 2 γ effects from the background variable to the latent variables, and 1 ϕ variance of the background variable. Because there are 15 (5 × 6/2) observed variances and covariances after inclusion of the background variable, the model is overidentified with 1 degree of freedom.

The Three-Wave Three-Variable Model

The final strategy for identifying and estimating models that include correlated measurement errors is to collect at least one additional wave of information. When two indicators of a latent variable are measured in three waves, all parameters linking the latent variables to the indicators, stability coefficients of the latent variables, and measurement error in indicators at adjacent waves may be estimated without constraint. In that case, there are 21 observed variances and covariances, and 18 free parameters, so the model as a whole can be tested with 3 degrees of freedom. The only limitation in this model is that correlations between the measurement error of indicators at waves 1 and 3 are not identified without further constraint. One reasonable constraint is that the measurement error covariances in adjacent waves are equal, and under this assumption the measurement errors linking wave 1 and wave 3 indicators are identified as well. Alternatively, the value of the θ_ϵ could be set equal across waves, but this restriction is less plausible, as was shown in the single-indicator models discussed above.

When three indicators for the latent variable are measured at three or more points in time, a model with correlated errors in nonadjacent waves may be estimated without constraint. This model also allows more sophisticated modeling and interpretation of the correlated measurement errors than is possible with fewer wave panel data. Jagodzinski et al. (1987) and Raffolovich and Bohrnstedt (1987), for example, show how models with correlated measurement error correspond directly with the classical factor analytic model in which each observed variable is a function of a common factor (the latent variable), unique error variance, and a specific item factor, which measures variance specific to the item that is neither random measurement error nor related to the common factor. The item factor thus incorporates the over-time error correlations between measurement errors discussed above. In cross-sectional analyses, the specific item variance is merged with the unique random error component, thus overestimating the pure error component of an indicator (Raffolovich & Bohrnstedt, 1987, p. 386). With multiwave panel data, a model depicted in Figure 4.4 may be estimated in order to distinguish the three sources of variation in particular items.

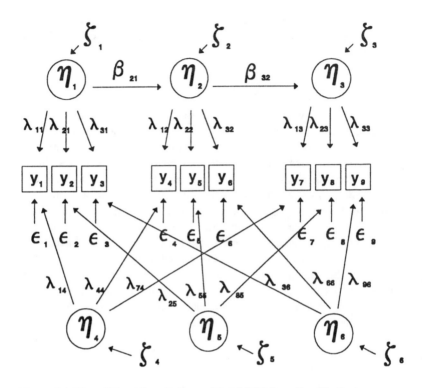

Figure 4.4. Three-Wave Three-Indicator Model With Item-Specific Factors

In this model, each indicator y_k is caused by a common factor (latent variable η_1 for the first wave, η_2 for the second wave, and η_3 for the third wave), an error term ϵ_k, as well as by a specific item factor (η_4 for the first item in each wave, η_5 for the second item, and η_6 for the third). One λ coefficient, or factor loading, links each indicator to the latent variable of substantive interest, and another to the item factor at each point in time. The model assumes that the random error and structural disturbances are independent of the latent variables and the specific factors, and also assumes that the specific and common factors are independent of one another.

To specify the simple correlated error models estimated earlier in LIS-REL, one needed only to free the covariances between the ϵ_k in adjacent waves. With the specific factors included here, the LISREL setup is somewhat more complex. The scale of each common factor η is set by fixing the coefficient of one of the indicators to be 1 in each wave, and the scale of the specific factor is set by fixing the coefficient linking each specific factor to an indicator in one of its waves to be 1 as well. These specific choices are arbitrary, but one indicator's coefficient must always be set to 1 for each latent variable, including the specific factors. Measurement error variances are specified as uncorrelated with one another because the loadings on the specific factors capture the over-time correlation of the same items. The model as presented in Figure 4.4 is overidentified with 16 degrees of freedom, as there are $9 \times 10/2$ or 45 observed variances and covariances, and 29 free parameters. Alternative models may also be estimated and compared by placing constraints on certain coefficients. For example, a model with no item-specific factors, a model with factor loadings linking the common factors to its individual indicators to be equal over time, and a model with factor loadings linking the specific factors to its individual indicators to be equal over time could all be tested and compared with one another. Whenever such models are nested within one another, that is, contain the same variables but with one or more constraints on the Λ or Θ_ϵ matrices, the improvement in fit may be assessed through the difference in χ^2 between the two models.

Once the results are obtained, it is also possible to decompose the variance in each indicator into its common, specific, and unique components. Raffolovich and Bohrnstedt (1987) show that when all latent variables, including the specific factors, are standardized to have a mean of zero and unit variance, the total variance in each indicator is estimated as

$$\hat{\sigma}^2(y) = \lambda_c^2 + \lambda_s^2 + \theta_\epsilon \qquad (4.15)$$

where "c" refers to the common factor and "s" to the specific factor. It is then straightforward to calculate the proportion of total item variance accounted for by the common factor, the specific factor, and the unique error variance.

Finally, the measurement effects in these models, as with all the models considered in this chapter, can be estimated in the context of more fully specified structural models as well. The advantage of this strategy is that bias in the estimates of the stabilities of latent variables will be reduced, and these differences may also affect the estimates of measurement error. Further, as the reason for correcting for measurement error in many analyses is to obtain unbiased estimates of the causal effects between latent variables, the simultaneous specification of measurement error and structural effects will best accomplish this goal.

5. SPURIOUS ASSOCIATION AND
AUTOCORRELATED DISTURBANCES

Previous chapters have described procedures for strengthening causal inference by estimating panel models with various lag structures and measurement error in the variables. Successful causal inference in the panel context, however, depends not only on specifying the proper lag structure and correcting for measurement error, but also on controlling for the potentially contaminating effects of outside unmeasured variables on a causal system. Unmeasured variables are the primary cause of *autocorrelation* in the structural disturbances of the endogenous variables, and failure to take this possibility into account will lead to biased OLS estimation of the causal effects in many static-score panel models. Although this is a common problem, panel data often contain enough information to begin to control for autocorrelation, and also to test for other possible patterns of spurious association between variables.

One panel model of spurious association builds directly on the measurement models discussed in the previous chapter.

Consider the relationship between involvement with delinquent peers (IDP) and self-reported delinquency (SRD) that we have investigated using the National Youth Survey. In Chapter 3 we saw how panel data assists in the estimation of possible reciprocal effects between these variables. But a plausible alternative model is that IDP and SRD are not really measuring distinct concepts; rather, they may both be indicators of a more general common factor, for example, an individual's overall behavioral orientation toward delinquency (Gottfredson & Hirschi, 1987). In such a model, the common factor "causes" responses toward both variables, and all covariation between the IDP and SRD scales would be explained by their association with the general common factor. Although there is no way to rule out the common factor model with cross-sectional data, with panel data the common factor model can be estimated and compared to a model with direct causal effects between variables.

In other instances, the common factor approach may be ruled out on theoretical grounds. For example, we might assume with good reason that candidate evaluations and party identification are not indicators of the same general concept, based on the well-documented theoretical distinctiveness of the two concepts. But the problem of spurious association remains because it is likely that other variables *not* included in the model still exert influence in the causal system. These variables would not be "latent" variables of a concept measured by party identification and candidate evaluations, but rather variables representing distinct factors that simply were omitted from the data collection or not considered by the researcher. These variables could be background social or demographic characteristics such as prior military service, prior voting behavior, or attitudinal factors such as evaluations of presidential performance that might be assumed to influence both party identification and evaluations of the competing candidates. In cross-sectional studies, these variables are lumped into the error terms of the endogenous variables and, to the extent that the unmeasured variables relate to party identification and candidate ratings, the estimated coefficients linking these variables will be biased. In panel studies, this problem is compounded whenever unmeasured variables have some stability over time; in that case, the structural disturbances of the endogenous variables will be autocorrelated and OLS estimation of model parameters will be incorrect. In static-score panel models, these unmeasured variables lead to bias in the estimates of the effects of lagged Y and possibly of the effects of X on Y as well.

This chapter presents some alternative methods for estimating common factor and unmeasured variable models with panel data. These models offer no foolproof means of controlling for spurious association between variables; they each entail their own set of assumptions that may or may not be plausible in a given research situation. Although the methods will not and cannot yield the confidence in causal inference possible with experimental designs, they do offer some much-needed aid in improving the quality of causal inference in nonexperimental settings.

Common Factor Models

The general two-wave, two-variable common factor model is shown in diagram form as Figure 5.1. In this model, there are no causal effects from X to Y or Y to X; the observed covariance between the two variables is a function of their joint relationship with the common factor Z at each point in time. Each X and Y variable is also caused by a random measurement error component e_i, which is assumed to be uncorrelated with Z. As should be apparent, the model is identical to the two-indicator, two-wave measurement model described in Chapter 4, with the dashed lines in the figure representing the possible correlations between the measurement errors of X and Y over time. The structural effects to be estimated in the model are those linking the common factor Z at times 1 and 2 to X_1 and X_2 (λ_1 and λ_2), from Z to Y_1 and Y_2 (λ_3 and λ_4), and the stability of Z (β_1). For ease

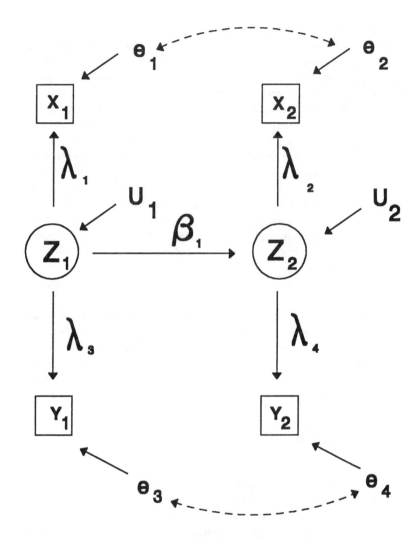

Figure 5.1. The Two-Wave Two-Variable Common Factor Model

of presentation, the X, Y, and Z here are assumed to be standardized variables. A variety of spurious common factor models based on different assumptions about the structural effects and measurement errors in Figure 5.1 can be tested against the data.

Two restrictive common factor models may be tested by simply comparing the magnitude of certain observed correlations. If it can be assumed that the causal effects linking Z with the X_i and Y_i are equal across waves, that is, $\lambda_1 = \lambda_2$ and $\lambda_3 = \lambda_4$, and that there are no correlated errors of measurement between X_1 and X_2, and Y_1 and Y_2, then the model leads to the prediction that the cross-lagged correlations between X_1 and Y_2, and Y_1 and X_2, will be equal (Kenny, 1973). As mentioned in Chapter 3, comparison of cross-lagged correlations has been rejected as a means of assessing the causal priority between variables (Duncan, 1969; Rogosa, 1979; Shingles, 1976), but its usefulness in testing this particular (although restrictive) spurious model remains. When no correlated errors of measurement exist but the effects from Z to its indicators X and Y are not equal across waves, then the relevant model test becomes

$$r(X_1X_2)r(Y_1Y_2) = r(X_1Y_2)r(X_2Y_1), \tag{5.1}$$

that is, whether the product of the over-time stability correlations of X and Y equals the product of the cross-lagged correlations.

These tests are usually incomplete, however, because of the strong presumption of correlated errors of measurement across panel waves. Common factor models that allow for the possibility of correlated errors may be specified and tested within the LISREL or related frameworks, following the identical procedures discussed for the two-wave two-variable measurement models in the previous chapter. The relationship between involvement with delinquent peers (IDP) and self-reported delinquency (SRD) in waves 1 and 2 of the National Youth Survey is used to illustrate these procedures.

The initial LISREL estimation of the model without correlated errors shows that it cannot account for the observed correlations between SRD and IDP over time. This model, which constrains the structural effects from Z_i to IDP and SRD over time to be equal, yields a very poor fit to the data, with a χ^2 of 161.3 with 3 degrees of freedom. Relaxing the equality constraint improves the model considerably and results in a χ^2 of 138.5 with 1 degree of freedom. This difference of 22.8 with 2 degrees of freedom is statistically significant, but still shows that the model as a whole fits the data very poorly. Thus both of these restrictive models may be rejected as explaining the relationship between SRD and IDP in the NYS data.

Unfortunately, a common factor model that includes correlated errors of measurement is underidentified, and more information is needed to estimate the structural parameters. One solution discussed in Chapter 4 was to add one more wave of observations, and the resultant three-wave, two-variable model will have enough observed correlations (15) with which to estimate the structural parameters. As was noted, however, only correlations of measurement errors between variables at adjacent waves will be identified without constraint; more indicators, or the imposition of equality constraints on certain parameters, are necessary to estimate error correlations between wave 1 and wave 3 variables. When only two waves of data are available, however, the addition of a background variable also achieves identification of all structural parameters and measurement error correlations without constraint. The model is overidentified with 1 degree of freedom with which the fit of the model can be tested.

In the present example, age is included as the observed background variable, and this model is reestimated including correlated errors between IDP_1 and IDP_2, and SRD_1 and SRD_2. The model fits the data better than the two previous specifications, with a χ^2 value with 1 degree of freedom of 4.9. Nevertheless, the goodness of fit is not sufficient to accept this model as holding in the population. By comparison, a model that specifies causal effects between IDP and SRD in accordance with the feedback process found earlier (synchronous effect from IDP to SRD in wave 2, cross-lagged effect from SRD in wave 1 to IDP in wave 2) fits the data extremely well and shows significant causal effects between IDP and SRD. In this instance, the rejection of the spurious common factor model gives added credence to the applicability of a model with direct causal effects between variables.

When the common factor model is not rejected, its estimated coefficients should be interpreted exactly as in the measurement models of the previous chapter. The effects from the Z_i to X_i and Y_i represent the loadings of these indicators onto the common factor, with β_1 representing the stability of the common factor over time. In models with background variables included, the γ coefficients represent the effect of the background variables on the common factor, and the correlation between measurement errors of the observed variables represents item-specific over-time variation in either X or Y that is unrelated to the common factor.

As in previous chapters, however, it should be emphasized that no model should be accepted on purely statistical grounds if the parameter estimates are unreasonable or imply substantive relationships that are theoretically untenable. The estimation process should always be supplemented by attention to the assumptions underlying each model, and whether they can be justified in a given situation. If the models do not fit the data or are theoretically unacceptable, alternative models, including those with direct causal effects, should then be tested and compared.

Unmeasured Variable Models

Spurious association between variables may be produced by another process aside from their joint relationship to a common factor. X and Y may be related because theoretically distinct unmeasured variables have been omitted or neglected from a given model. If certain assumptions about the form of these unmeasured variables can be justified, however, panel data may be used to estimate direct causal effects between variables of interest once the contaminating influences of the unmeasured variables are removed.

Let us assume that the true model explaining a given dependent variable Y_t is

$$Y_t = \beta_0 + \beta_1 X_t + \beta_2 Y_{t-1} + Z_t + \epsilon_t \tag{5.2}$$

where Z_t is an unmeasured variable that is unknown to the researcher or otherwise could not be included in the model, and ϵ_t is a random disturbance term. The incorrect estimation equation then becomes

$$Y_t = \beta_0 + \beta_1 X_t + \beta_2 Y_{t-1} + u_t \tag{5.3}$$

where

$$u_t = Z_t + \epsilon_t . \tag{5.4}$$

The presence of Z_t in the disturbance term u_t has several important consequences. First, the u_t necessarily will be correlated over time whenever the stability of Z_t is greater than zero. In other words, there will be *autocorrelation* in the structural disturbances of the endogenous variable Y over time. Second, if Z has nonzero stability, Y_{t-1} in Equation (5.3) necessarily will be correlated with u_t because of their joint association with Z_{t-1}. This means that OLS will no longer be appropriate for estimating the model, as the correlation between the disturbance term and the explanatory variable Y_{t-1} will lead to biased and inconsistent estimates of the model's parameters (Johnston, 1972). This typically results in OLS overestimation of the "true" effect of Y_{t-1} on Y_t, as some of the stability observed in Y is spurious because of the over-time stability of the omitted variable Z. Third, whenever the omitted variable Z_t is also correlated with X_t, additional bias may be introduced in the estimation of β_1 from Equation (5.3). In that case, the effect of X_t on Y_t in Equation (5.3) would be at least partially spurious because of their joint relationship with Z_t, and the severity of the bias would depend on the strength of Z's relationship with the two observed variables.

As opposed to time series analyses with a large number of observations over time, it is very difficult to correct for the biases caused by omitted variables in short-term panel studies with only a few waves of observations. The problem is most acute when the lagged endogenous variable appears as a predictor, because causal models will need to specify effects between both Y_{t-1} on Y_t and between u_{t-1} and u_t simultaneously. Obviously, the best strategy is to specify the substantive model as completely as possible so that the error term in a given equation is relatively small and so that the correlation between the errors that are generated by omitted variables is relatively harmless. But design limitations often render this strategy impractical, leaving several alternative options for estimating these models.

First, additional information in the form of outside *observed* variables may be included in the model, and the parameters from Equation (5.3) may be recovered through an instrumental variable-type estimation procedure. Second, different assumptions about the stability of the omitted variable Z may be made that give rise to certain expected patterns of covariation between the structural disturbances. The parameters in Equation (5.3) may then be recovered in multiwave panel analyses by imposing constraints on the covariances of the disturbance terms and estimating the model in LISREL or related procedures. Third, additional unmeasured variables may be *explicitly* specified within the LISREL framework and, given enough information in the form of observed correlations, a variety of models can be estimated that include structural effects between X and Y as well as the effects of Z on each variable over time. Each of these methods is illustrated using the empirical examples analyzed thus far in the monograph.

Instrumental Variables Estimation

One solution to the problem of autocorrelated errors in Equation (5.3) involves using additional information in the form of an instrumental variable that satisfies the conditions outlined in previous chapters: (a) it is related to Y_{t-1} but uncorrelated with u_t and (b) it has no direct causal effect on Y_t. The first condition guarantees that the instrument will be unrelated to the equation's disturbance, and the second condition ensures that the model will be identified. If such an instrument is available, Two Stage Least Squares or maximum likelihood methods may be used to obtain consistent estimates of the parameters in Equation (5.3).

For example, omitted variables that influenced legal protest potential and group memberships in 1987 and 1989 may have given rise to autocorrelated disturbances in the models considered in previous chapters. The static-score equations can be estimated predicting protest and group membership in 1989 only if an instrumental variable or set of variables exists for the two lagged dependent variables, legal protest potential and group memberships in 1987. If it can be assumed that *illegal* protest potential in 1987 (Z_1) influences legal protest potential in 1987, has no direct causal effect on legal protest potential in 1989 once other variables are controlled, and is unrelated to legal protest potential's 1989 structural disturbance term, then it may be used as an instrumental variable for legal protest potential in 1987. The TSLS estimation would proceed as in earlier chapters: Regress Y_{t-1} on its instrument and all other exogenous variables to generate $\hat{Y}_{t-1}$, and then regress Y_t on $\hat{Y}_{t-1}$ and all other variables in Y_t's predictive equation.

The situation is complicated somewhat whenever autocorrelated disturbances due to an omitted Z exist in the context of a reciprocal effects model, that is, when the Y in Equation (5.3) also influence X. In that case, X as well as Y_{t-1} will necessarily be correlated with u_t, and an additional instrumental variable will need to be included in the model (Hannan & Young, 1977). In the present instance, we assume that membership in groups that encourage *illegal* protest (Z_2) at time 1 is unrelated to the structural disturbances at time 2, and this may be used as an instrument for GROUPS in a reciprocal effects model.

Within the LISREL framework, the estimation of these kinds of models is a straightforward extension of those estimated previously. The relevant covariances between structural disturbance terms are specified in the Ψ matrix, and if PROTEST$_1$, PROTEST$_2$, GROUPS$_1$, and GROUPS$_2$ were endogenous variables 1 through 4, the parameters ψ_{21} and ψ_{43} would be freed to allow for the possibility of autocorrelation. The instrumental variables are treated as exogenous ξ variables and their effects specified in the Γ matrix containing the structural effects between exogenous and endogenous variables. Constraints are then placed on certain γ effects in this matrix to identify the model: For example, the effect of 1987 illegal protest potential on 1989 PROTEST$_2$ would be constrained to be zero, as would the effect of 1987 membership in groups encouraging illegal protest on 1989 GROUPS$_2$. The remaining effects and matrices would be specified exactly as in previous chapters, depending on the precise structural and measurement processes that are hypothesized to govern the causal system.

Assuming the three-indicator measurement model for PROTEST$_1$ and PROTEST$_2$ from the previous chapter, and the "feedback model" uncovered there for the structural effects between GROUPS and PROTEST over time, the autocorrelation model is estimated using LISREL maximum likelihood methods, and the following results are obtained for the structural portion of the model:

$$\text{PROTEST}_2 = \begin{array}{l} .32 \text{ PROTEST}_1 \\ (.09) \\ \underline{.29} \end{array} + \begin{array}{l} 1.17 \text{ GROUPS}_2 \\ (.15) \\ \underline{.46} \end{array} \qquad (5.5)$$

$$\text{GROUPS}_2 = \begin{array}{l} .95 \text{ GROUPS}_1 \\ (.16) \\ \underline{.86} \end{array} + \begin{array}{l} -.01 \text{ PROTEST}_1 \\ (.05) \\ \underline{-.03} \end{array}$$

The covariance between the disturbance terms of PROTEST$_1$ and PROTEST$_2$ is estimated to have a statistically insignificant value of .25, with a standardized value of .05, whereas the covariance between the error terms for GROUPS$_1$ and GROUPS$_2$ is estimated to be −.25, with a standardized value of −.34. This estimate of the covariance between structural disturbances is statistically significant. Comparing the estimated reciprocal effects between protest and group memberships in this model with the no-autocorrelation model from Equation (4.14) shows that the relationship here is entirely unidirectional, with GROUPS influencing PROTEST. The stability effects of PROTEST and especially GROUPS differs considerably, and this finding is a direct result of the *large negative* value for the estimated covariance between the disturbance terms for the GROUPS variables over time.

Panel models that estimate autocorrelated disturbances, either through Two Stage Least Squares or LISREL-type methods, frequently find such patterns of negative autocorrelation (Long, 1983b, p. 78; Markus, 1979, p. 53). Although there may be instances where negative autocorrelation could be given a substantive interpretation, it is more likely that the model is misspecified. One strong possibility is that the assumption that the variables (here GROUPS$_1$ and GROUPS$_2$) are measured without error is erroneous. The presence of measurement error leads to the same problem for OLS estimation as does autocorrelation, namely a correlation between the independent variables and the error term of its equation. And because one solution to the problem of measurement error is also to include instrumental variables in the analysis, it is often the case that structural effects are dissattenuated as they are in measurement models once this bias is controlled.[16] Hence models should be interpreted cautiously when findings of negative autocorrelation emerge, and additional models proposed that correct for measurement error or other misspecifications.

With two waves of observations, the instrumental variable procedure is the only means available to begin to control for the problem of autocorrelated disturbances. But the underlying assumptions about the instrumental variables' exogeneity and effects on the other variables in the system often may not be tenable. In the present example, it may be implausible to assume that *illegal protest potential* in 1987 is related to legal protest in 1987 but has no effect on legal protest in 1989 and is also unrelated to any omitted variable Z in legal protest potential's error term in 1989. Further, the substitution of the instrumental variable for the lagged endogenous variable generally results in much less precision in the second-stage estimates of all causal effects. These problems show that the instrumental variables approach in many cases will be unsatisfactory as a means of controlling for the confounding effects of omitted variables in the causal system. With three or more waves of data, the methods described below usually will be preferred.

Assumptions About the Stability of the Unmeasured Variable

Another method for estimating causal effects in the presence of autocorrelated disturbances is based on different assumptions that can be made about the stability of the omitted variable in the error term of Equation (5.4). In short-term panel studies, it is often reasonable to assume that Z represents some individual or unit-specific characteristic or characteristics that are constant over time, so that $Z_{t-1} = Z_t = Z$. The error structure of Equation (5.4) then becomes

$$u_t = Z + \epsilon_t \qquad (5.6)$$

where ϵ_t is a random disturbance. Given this assumption, the correlation between the error terms u_t in Equation (5.3) will be a constant value no matter what the lag, that is, the correlation between the error terms at times 1 and 2 will be identical to that between the error terms at times 1 and 3, 2 and 3, 1 and 4, and so on. In longer-term panel studies, the omitted variables may be more likely to display less than perfect stability over time, in which case the structure of the error term will follow the first-order autoregressive scheme commonly seen in time series research:

$$u_t = \rho u_{t-1} + \epsilon_t \qquad (5.7)$$

where ρ is the autocorrelation parameter with a value less than 1, and ϵ_t is as above. Given this error structure, the correlation between error terms at successive lags decays in a geometric fashion, with adjacent disturbances correlated with value ρ, disturbances two lags apart correlated with value ρ^2, and so on.

Tuma and Hannan (1984) and Stimson (1985) outline methods within the framework of pooled cross-section and time series analysis for estimating these types of panel models with autocorrelated error structures. The pooling approach can be an appropriate analytical strategy for three-wave and multiwave data when the causal structure of the model is constant over time and when the time period between waves of observation is equally spaced. The main drawback to these methods in the autocorrelation models considered here is that, as noted above, additional information in the form of instrumental variables must be included whenever the two variables are presumed to influence one another in a reciprocal causal model.

Autocorrelation models in nonpooled multiwave panels also may be estimated within the LISREL framework, although there are few exemplars in the literature. The estimation would proceed as in the two-wave case by freeing the off-diagonal elements in the Ψ matrix of structural disturbances and then by imposing constraints on the individual ψ elements depending on the assumptions about the structure of the disturbance terms. In a standardized three-wave model, three disturbance correlations for the Y endogenous variable would be freed: ψ_{21}, representing the correlation between the disturbances of Y at waves 1 and 2; ψ_{32}, representing the correlation between the waves 2 and 3 disturbances; and ψ_{31}, representing the correlations between the waves 1 and 3 disturbances. Similar parameters representing the correlations of the X variable's error term over time would also be freed. Finally, the model with constant omitted variables can be estimated by constraining all correlations between the disturbances of the endogenous variables to equal one another, that is,[17]

$$\psi_{21} = \psi_{32} = \psi_{31}. \qquad (5.8)$$

Table 5.1 shows the parameter estimates from two models with and without correlated structural disturbances using the 1980 party identification and candidate evaluation relationship analyzed in previous chapters. As usual, a cross-lagged specification of causal effects is assumed, and the cross-lagged effects are constrained from PID to THERM from waves 1 and 2, and waves 2 and 3, to equal one another. Similar constraints are placed on the effects of THERM to PID, the stability effects of PID and THERM over time, and the error correlations are constrained for PID and THERM as in Equation (5.8) to model the autocorrelated disturbances produced by stable omitted variables.

The initial model (1) specifies autocorrelated disturbances but no measurement error for either variable over time. The results show very high estimated stabilities of party identification and the thermometer scale, and a statistically significant cross-lagged effect in only one direction, from PARTY to THERM. As in the two-wave model, however, the estimates of autocorrelation are negative and statistically significant, indicating probable model misspecification. Given the pattern of results in the previous chapter, it is likely that the assumption of no measurement error in model (1) is erroneous. Model (2) reestimates this same model with the three-wave single-indicator measurement error structure from Chapter 4 and includes autocorrelated disturbances. The results show that both autocorrelation parameters are now very small in magnitude and statistically insignificant, whereas the stability and cross-lagged effects are similar to the results found in Chapter 4. In addition, the model as a whole has a far better fit to the data than the no-measurement error model in (1). Confidence in the unidirectional causal influence between party identification and candidate thermometer ratings during the 1980 campaign is therefore strengthened because the pattern of effects remained similar across a number of models with different assumptions about the presence of autocorrelation and measurement error in the causal system. Moreover, in this example, the problem of measurement error appeared to have greater consequences for the estimates of causal effects than the confounding effects of autocorrelation. Nevertheless, the potential errors in causal inference due to autocorrelation are serious, and the analyst should attempt to verify the pattern of causal results with a variety of alternative model specifications whenever possible.

If the error structure is assumed to follow a first-order autoregressive pattern as in Equation (5.7) above, then the LISREL estimation would proceed in a standardized model by freeing the disturbance correlations, setting the covariances between adjacent disturbance terms to equal one

TABLE 5.1
Three-Wave Models With and Without Autocorrelated Disturbances

	Model	
	(1)	*(2)*
Stabilities		
Party Identification	1.0	.99
	(.02)	(.03)
Thermometer Ratings	.80	.71
	(.05)	(.07)
Cross-Lagged Effects		
Party-Thermometer	.13	.20
	(.03)	(.04)
Thermometer-Party	−.02	.01
	(.02)	(.01)
Autocorrelated Disturbances		
Party Identification	−.13	−.003
	(.01)	(.03)
Thermometer Ratings	−.09	.05
	(.03)	(.04)
Synchronous Disturbance Correlation		
Party Identification-Thermometer Ratings	.04	.03
	(.01)	(.01)
Measurement Error Variance		
Party Identification	—	.13
Estimated Reliability		(.03)
		.87
Thermometer Ratings		.20
Estimated Reliability		(.04)
		.80
χ^2 (df)	71.3 (7)	9.8 (5)
	$p < .001$	$p = .08$

SOURCE: National Election Study, Major Panel File, 1980.
NOTE: Entries are standardized maximum likelihood estimates; standard errors in parentheses.
N for all models is 733.

another, and then setting the covariances between disturbances at times 1 and 3 to equal the product of the disturbance covariation at times 1 and 2 and the disturbance covariation at times 2 and 3. Methods for specifying models with such constraints on parameters within LISREL can be found in Hayduk (1987). Finally, LISREL models that allow unconstrained estimation of the disturbance covariances can be specified if there is enough information available to identify these parameters. In reciprocal effects models, however, unconstrained estimation of these correlations often will not be possible; moreover, such ad hoc model specification will not reflect any known structure of the error terms.

Explicit Modeling of the Unmeasured Variable

A final method for estimating models with omitted variables within the LISREL or other structural modeling frameworks is to specify explicitly an additional latent variable that has no observed indicators to stand for the *unmeasured* variable Z in the causal model. With at least three waves of observation, models can be estimated that include structural effects between X and Y as well as effects from the "phantom" variable Z. The main advantage of this approach is that it allows for the direct specification of the assumed interrelationships between measured and unmeasured variables in the causal system and, given enough degrees of freedom with which to identify the parameters, provides the most detailed estimates of the magnitude and direction of all causal effects. One possible unmeasured variable model of this type is shown in Figure 5.2, where a single omitted variable Z (modeled in LISREL as an additional η with no observed indicator) influences both X and Y over time, and X and Y have cross-lagged effects on one another as well.

In order to identify this model, the structural effects must be constrained to be equal over time, as must the error variances for the Y_2 and Y_3 equations, and the X_2 and X_3 equations. The variance of the unobserved variable Z is set to 1. As in other cross-lagged models estimated thus far, a synchronous covariation between disturbances between the time 2 variables and between the time 3 variables is included to capture omitted factors that may influence responses to both X and Y in one wave but not the next. Given this specification, the model is overidentified with 7 degrees of freedom. With more waves of observation, fewer restrictions on the parameters will need to be made. It should also be noted that this model can be extended very easily to include *observed* outside variables that mutually influence X and Y as well. In actual practice, these variables would

84

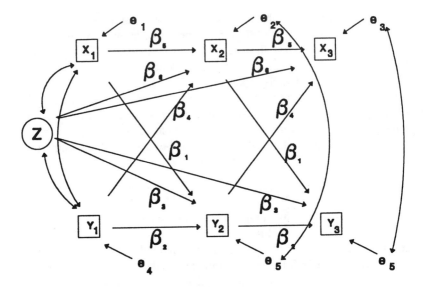

Figure 5.2. Three-Wave Cross-Lagged Model With Unmeasured Variable Z

be treated as exogenous influences on all six variables in Figure 5.2, rendering the model a representation of potential spuriousness caused by both the measured and the unmeasured outside variables. For illustrative purposes, these variables are omitted from consideration here. This model is estimated using the self-reported delinquency (SRD)-involvement with delinquent peers (IDP) relationship analyzed previously. Results are shown in Table 5.2.

The model as a whole fits the data rather poorly, with a χ^2 value of 90.8 with 7 degrees of freedom ($p < .001$). However, it should be recalled that the model with reciprocal synchronous and cross-lagged effects between SRD and IDP in Chapter 3 yielded a χ^2 value of 167.0 with 8 degrees of freedom, indicating that the unmeasured variable model has a better fit to the data than a model with only direct causal effects. Interestingly, the model shows that once the effects of the unmeasured variable are controlled, there are no significant cross-lagged effects in either direction between SRD and IDP. Reestimation of the unmeasured variable model with a synchronous effect from IDP to SRD and a lagged effect from SRD to IDP, however, yields a model χ^2 of 101.8 with 8 degrees of freedom, approximately the same fit to the data as the cross-lagged model above. In this

TABLE 5.2.
Three-Wave Unmeasured Variable Model for
Self-Reported Delinquency and Involvement With Delinquent Peers

Structural Effects	
SRD to SRD	.40
IDP to IDP	.14
IDP to SRD	−.04*
SRD to IDP	.01*
Z to SRD	.45
Z to IDP	.58
Time 1 Correlations	
r(SRD, IDP)	.54
r(SRD, Z)	.61
r(IDP, Z)	.63
r(IDP, SRD disturbances)	.13
χ^2 (df)	90.8 (7)
Probability	< .001

SOURCE: 1976-1978 National Youth Survey.
NOTE: N = 1,725. All variables are standardized, and entries are maximum likelihood estimates. All coefficients are significant at the .05 level except those starred.

"feedback" model, the standardized effect of IDP to SRD is significant with a value of .31, whereas the standardized effect of SRD to IDP is .10, a weaker value than in the models estimated in Chapter 3. These two models cannot be directly compared with three-wave data because a model with an unmeasured variable *and* with synchronous causal effects and synchronous disturbance correlations between X and Y is not identified.

Nevertheless, the results should give pause to the claim that reciprocal effects of similar magnitude exist between the two variables. The data are at least equally consistent with the interpretation that the relationship is overwhelmingly unidirectional or that it is fully spurious. In this case, because the fit of the models is poor, alternative specifications that allow for the possibility of measurement error in the observed variables should also be estimated and compared. Given more information in the form of additional waves of observation, models may be specified that can test all these interpretations against one another more definitely, along with models that include multiple unmeasured variables and possible change in the unmeasured variables over time.

This chapter has outlined certain models of spurious association and autocorrelation produced by common factors and unobserved variables. If significant causal effects exist between variables once these possible sources of spuriousness are controlled, then the researcher would have greater confidence in the validity of the results. However, it should be stressed that spurious association produced by *observed* variables is also an important problem in panel designs, and these kinds of effects can and should be tested against the data before drawing causal conclusions. Obviously, all observed variables that are theoretically linked to X and Y should always be included in the models. In addition, models that omit all direct causal effects between the variables of interest can be estimated and compared against causal effects models in terms of fit and substantive plausibility. Covariation between X and Y could be produced by observed third variables or by the synchronous covariation between disturbance terms, not by direct causal effects. Because the causal effects models are nested within models with *no* causal effects, their relative fit may be assessed in LISREL or related procedures through the difference in χ^2 test.

All of these methods should serve as complementary tools to test for spurious association, and it should be emphasized that estimating models with common factors and unobserved variables should not replace the more certain means available to researchers, namely, the direct inclusion of variables thought to be relevant in a given causal system. But the models here at least make some effort to incorporate the effects of unmeasured variables explicitly into the design, instead of simply assuming (as is done with cross-sectional data) that all relevant variables have been included. Moreover, the LISREL approach allows great flexibility in testing models against one another to determine the particular form of spurious association that may be present. In many cases, spurious association can be ruled out through these tests; but if not, then estimates from direct causal effects models should be viewed with caution and interpreted in light of the fact that common factor or unobserved variable models fit the data equally well.

6. CONCLUDING NOTE ON CAUSAL INFERENCE IN PANEL ANALYSIS

This monograph has reviewed multiple ways of strengthening the causal inference process through the analysis of panel data. Panel data may be used to estimate models that contain a variety of lag specifications, reciprocal causation, and measurement error; models that attempt to control for potentially spurious association between variables can be estimated as well. We showed throughout the monograph that the estimation and comparison of all of these models is greatly facilitated by the presence of three or more waves of panel data, but even two-wave panels offer significant advantages over cross-sectional data in overcoming common impediments to successful causal inference.

Although the analysis of panel data has important advantages over cross-sectional and other observational research designs, it has been stressed throughout the monograph that panel data cannot solve definitively all the difficult problems in causal inference in empirical research. All of the procedures and models developed here depend on their own set of assumptions, which in particular situations may be untenable or may yield implausible empirical results. The analyst should always be aware that because different models can be estimated that may fit a given set of data, no single model is the only one that can be accepted in a particular research situation. As Dwyer (1983) notes:

> The beginning of wisdom in causal inference from passive longitudinal data is the realization that an accepted model is only as good as the generality of the models that can be rejected by the same data. (p. 322)

The process of causal inference should not, then, be a simple matter of specifying and testing the effects that one wants to prove; rather it should proceed by attempting to reject a variety of plausible models, including those with no causal effects and those that test direct causal hypotheses. This is an extremely challenging task for which panel analysis offers the most promising, although imperfect, tools presently available for nonexperimental research.

APPENDIX:
LISREL Matrices and Notation

In LISREL structural models, endogenous variables are referred to with the greek letter η, exogenous variables as ξ, and the structural disturbances as ζs. Structural effects linking endogenous η variables with one another are labelled as β coefficients, whereas structural effects linking exogenous (or predetermined) ξ variables to endogenous variables are labelled as γ coefficients. For example, a simple three-wave model with one variable influencing itself over time may be written as

$$\eta_1 = \gamma_{11}\xi_1 + \zeta_1$$

$$\eta_2 = \beta_{21}\eta_1 + \zeta_2$$

(A.1)

where ξ_1 corresponds to the wave 1 (predetermined) value of the variable, and η_1 and η_2 to its wave 2 and wave 3 values, respectively. In matrix form, this system would look like

$$\begin{pmatrix} \eta_1 \\ \eta_2 \end{pmatrix} = \begin{pmatrix} 0 & 0 \\ \beta_{21} & 0 \end{pmatrix} \begin{pmatrix} \eta_1 \\ \eta_2 \end{pmatrix} + \begin{pmatrix} \gamma_{11} \\ 0 \end{pmatrix} \xi_1 + \begin{pmatrix} \zeta_1 \\ \zeta_2 \end{pmatrix}$$

The general multiequation matrix form of the LISREL structural equation system is

$$\eta = B\eta + \Gamma\xi + \zeta$$

(A.2)

where η is a vector of m endogenous variables, ξ is a vector of n exogenous variables, B is an $(m \times m)$ matrix of the β coefficients linking the endogenous variables, Γ is an $(m \times n)$ matrix of the γ coefficients linking the exogenous variables to the endogenous variables, and ζ is an $(m \times 1)$ vector of structural disturbances. The other relevant matrices for purposes of estimation are Φ, an $(n \times n)$ matrix of variances and covariances of the exogenous variables, and Ψ, an $(m \times m)$ matrix of the variances and covariances of the structural disturbance terms.

When the variables contain random measurement error, this procedure is extended by expressing the set of both measurement and structural equations of a model in matrix form. If η is the true score for an endogenous variable, and λ_y is the regression coefficient linking the true score to the observed indicator y, the multiequation matrix form of the measurement model is

$$y = \Lambda_y \eta + \epsilon \qquad (A.3)$$

where y is a $(q \times 1)$ vector of q indicators of the endogenous variables, Λ_y is a $(q \times m)$ matrix of the λ_y linkages between the m endogenous variables and the indicators, and ϵ is a $(q \times 1)$ vector of the measurement error in the indicators. The variances and covariances of the measurement errors are summarized in a $(q \times q)$ matrix Θ_ϵ, with individual elements θ_ϵ.

When models contain exogenous variables, an identical set of measurement equations can be written for each of their indicators. The equivalent equation for A.3 is

$$x = \Lambda_x \xi + \delta \qquad (A.4)$$

where x is a $(p \times 1)$ vector of p indicators of the exogenous ξ variables, Λ_x is a $(p \times n)$ matrix of the λ_x linkages between the n exogenous variables and the indicators, and δ is a $(p \times 1)$ vector of the measurement error in the indicators. The variances and covariances of the measurement errors for indicators of the exogenous variables are summarized in a $(p \times p)$ matrix Θ_δ, with individual elements θ_δ.

NOTES

1. These characteristics of panels are also found in another form of longitudinal data, "pooled time series data," which combine the time series of multiple units into a single data set (Sayrs, 1989). Although there is no formal difference between the two types of data, pooled time series are typically viewed as having a larger number of time points relative to units than do panels, which usually contain between two to five "waves" of data for a large number of cases. This distinction has given rise to differences in strategies for analyzing the two types of data (Kessler & Greenberg, 1981, Chapter 11; Tuma & Hannan, 1984, Chapter 2).

2. See Allison (1990) and Judd and Kenny (1981) for discussion of the conditions under which the unconditional change-score model is appropriate in the analysis of experimental and quasi-experimental data.

3. Hargens, Raskin, and Allison (1976, pp. 454-455), in an analysis of scientific productivity, state that a model without lagged Y "seems particularly appropriate for variables . . . which must be created or produced anew for each time interval, in contrast to variables which have an internal principle of stability, i.e., which tend to remain the same unless acted upon from without."

4. Other theoretical models including lagged Y as an independent variable are the *adaptive expectations* and *Koyck distributed lag* models. In the adaptive expectations model, the actual value of the dependent variable is determined by an unknown "antici-pated" value of the independent variable, rather than the actual value, and the model specifies that the anticipated value is created by correcting the prior period's anticipated value by a constant fraction of the difference between the last period's anticipated and actual values. In the Koyck model, present values of Y are determined by the present and all prior values of X. Algebraic manipulations of these models produce estimation equations with the same general form as the partial adjustment model, except that the error terms have different structures and present different problems for statistical estimation. See Gujarati (1988) for more detailed treatment of these models and their associated estimation procedures.

5. As Plewis (1985, p. 60) notes, "the causal link between $[X_t$ and $Y_t]$ . . . implies not so much a simultaneous effect as the possibility that a change in X at some time after occasion 1 leads to a change in y by occasion 2, although 'some time' is not defined in any precise way."

6. Because each of the X_1, X_2, and ΔX variables is a linear combination of the other two, it is not possible to include all three variables in the same regression model to estimate their unique effects. Kessler and Greenberg (1981, Chapter 6) suggest some procedures for estimating all three effects by making some highly restrictive assumptions about the magnitude of the effects or their interrelationships, or by introducing more information into the causal system.

7. The consistency of the two estimates can also be used as a test of the model as a whole. Tuma and Hannan (1984, p. 344) note that if the two estimates are widely divergent, it may indicate either a misspecification of the functional form of the original

differential equation, or a misspecification of the way that the exogenous variable X changes over time.

8. The TSLS routine in SPSS and other computer packages provides estimates of the structural disturbances from each equation, and the standardized covariance between U_1 and U_2 is simply the correlation between these estimates. If the synchronous model is estimated through maximum likelihood procedures in LISREL, then the 1 degree of freedom in the model allows a formal statistical test of the model's assumption. If the χ^2 value is larger than 3.84 (the critical value for 1 df at the .05 significance level), this indicates that the assumption of zero disturbance covariation does not hold in the population. Freeing this parameter, however, results in an unidentified model unless additional exogenous variables are included.

9. Gillespie and Fox's discussion is technically limited to what they refer to as "parallel" simultaneous equation models, which represent the reciprocal effects of the *same* variables measured for different units, for example, where the occupational aspirations of an adolescent and the occupational aspirations of his or her best friend are reciprocally related. In these instances especially, negative covariation between structural disturbances is theoretically highly unlikely; but the "consequences of random error in the measures of both the endogenous and exogenous variables and the consequences of omitting the cross-effects of a set of exogenous variables . . . (likely) . . . applies to all non-recursive models" (Gillespie & Fox, 1980, p. 304).

10. A related complication for three-wave models that are identified through consistency constraints is that the method depends on the causal system not being *in* equilibrium during the time span of the panel. If that were the case, the additional waves of observation would provide no new information regarding covariances between variables because the wave 2-wave 3 covariances necessarily would equal the wave 1-wave 2 values. Hence the models would be empirically underidentified. Kessler and Greenberg (1981, pp. 37-46) show that systems should be fairly far from equilibrium for the consistency approach to generate precise parameter estimates.

11. In standardized measurement models, the variance of η_t is fixed to equal 1, so that the λ_{kt} is a free parameter. If the observed indicators are also standardized, then the λ_{kt} represent the correlation between the latent variable and the observed indicator, which is sometimes referred to as an "epistemic correlation" or a "validity coefficient" (Sullivan & Feldman, 1979).

12. When random error is present in the dependent variable, OLS estimation of an independent variable's effect will yield unbiased yet inefficient estimates, as the estimated structural disturbance of the equation will be inflated. See Berry and Feldman (1985, pp. 27-28).

13. If $y_t = \lambda_{tt}\eta_t + \epsilon_t$, and if all variables are standardized, then squaring this expression and taking expectations yields $1 = \lambda_{tt}^2 + \sigma_{\epsilon_t}^2$, and the variance of the error term equals $1 - \lambda_{tt}^2$.

14. Werts et al. (1971), however, show that without making the assumption of equal error variance in the Wiley and Wiley model, the error variance of the "inner" indicator y_2 is identified, and thus its reliability may be calculated as $\rho_{y_t y_t} = r_{12} r_{23}/r_{13}$. But the remaining parameters are not identified without further constraints.

15. The table shows a "completely standardized solution" with the variances of both the latent variables and observed indicators standardized to 1. LISREL also produces a standardized solution with only the latent variable variances standardized to 1. If the latter solution is used, then the reliability of each indicator is calculated as $\lambda^2/[\lambda^2 + \text{Var}(\epsilon)]$.

16. In three-wave or multiwave models, other possible misspecifications are the omission of a causal parameter from the lagged endogenous variable in wave 1 to the endogenous variable in wave 3, the omission of a second-order autocorrelation effect from ϵ_1 to ϵ_3, or other misspecifications of the structure of the error terms. Any of these patterns could also bias upwards the stability effect of the lagged endogenous variable, which would be reflected in models without these effects as negative autocorrelation. These effects could be included and tested in LISREL, given sufficient degrees of freedom in the model.

17. There may be some bias in a three-wave model of this sort because the time 1 disturbances contain *all* of the variation in the time 1 variables, whereas the times 2 and 3 disturbances contain only *residual* variation. With four or more waves of data the assumption of equal covariances or correlations can be specified between the disturbance terms at times 2, 3, 4, and so on.

REFERENCES

ALLISON, P. D. (1990) "Change scores as dependent variables in regression analysis." In C. C. Clogg (Ed.), *Sociological Methodology 1990* (pp. 93-114). Oxford: Basil Blackwell.

ARMINGER, G. (1986) "Linear stochastic differential equation models for panel data with unobserved variables." In N. B. Tuma (Ed.), *Sociological Methodology 1986* (pp. 187-212). San Francisco: Jossey-Bass.

ARMINGER, G. (1987) "Misspecification, asymptotic stability, and ordinal variables in the analysis of panel data." *Sociological Methods & Research* 15: 336-348.

ASHER, H. B. (1983) *Causal Modeling.* Sage University Paper series on Quantitative Applications in the Social Sciences, 07-003. Beverly Hills, CA: Sage.

BENTLER, P. M. (1985) *Theory and Implementation of EQS: A Structural Equations Program.* Los Angeles: BMDP Statistical Software, Inc.

BERRY, W. D. (1984) *Nonrecursive Causal Models.* Sage University Paper series on Quantitative Applications in the Social Sciences, 07-037. Beverly Hills, CA: Sage.

BERRY, W. D., and FELDMAN, S. (1985) *Multiple Regression in Practice.* Sage University Paper series on Quantitative Applications in the Social Sciences, 07-050. Beverly Hills, CA: Sage.

BOHRNSTEDT, G. W. (1969) "Observations on the measurement of change." In E. F. Borgatta (Ed.), *Sociological Methodology 1969* (pp. 113-136). San Francisco: Jossey-Bass.

BOLLEN, K. (1989) *Structural Equations With Latent Variables.* New York: Wiley.

CARMINES, E. G., and ZELLER, R. (1979) *Reliability and Validity Assessment.* Sage University Paper series on Quantitative Applications in the Social Sciences, 07-017. Beverly Hills, CA: Sage.

COLEMAN, J. S. (1968) "The mathematical study of change." In H. Blalock and A. Blalock (Eds.), *Methodology in Social Research* (pp. 428-478). New York: McGraw-Hill.

COSTNER, H. L. (1969) "Theory, deduction, and the rules of correspondence." *American Journal of Sociology* 75: 245-263.

DUNCAN, O. D. (1969) "Some linear models for two wave, two variable panel analysis." *Psychological Bulletin* 72: 177-82.

DWYER, J. H. (1983) *Statistical Models for the Social and Behavioral Sciences.* New York: Oxford University Press.

ELLIOTT, D. S., HUIZINGA, D. H., and AGETON, S. S. (1985) *Explaining Delinquency and Drug Use.* Beverly Hills, CA: Sage.

FELDMAN, S. (1989) "The reliability and stability of policy positions: Evidence from a five-wave panel study." In J. A. Stimson (Ed.), *Political Analysis Volume 1* (pp. 25-60). Ann Arbor: University of Michigan Press.

FINKEL, S. E. (1993) "Reexamining the 'minimal effects' model in recent presidential elections." *Journal of Politics* 55: 1-21.

94

FINKEL, S. E., MULLER, E. N., and OPP, K.-D. (1989) "Personal influence, collective rationality, and mass political action." *American Political Science Review* 83: 885-903.

GILLESPIE, M. W., and FOX, J. (1980) "Specification error and negatively correlated disturbances in 'parallel' simultaneous-equation models." *Sociological Methods & Research* 8: 273-308.

GOTTFREDSON, M., and HIRSCHI, T. (1987) "The methodological adequacy of longitudinal research on crime and delinquency." *Criminology* 25: 581-614.

GREEN, D., and PALMQUIST, B. (1990) "Of artifacts and partisan stability." *American Journal of Political Science* 34: 872-902.

GUJARATI, D. (1988) *Basic Econometrics*. New York: McGraw-Hill.

HANNAN, M. T., and YOUNG, A. A. (1977) "Estimation in panel models: Results on pooling cross-sections and time series." In D. R. Heise (Ed.), *Sociological Methodology 1977* (pp. 52-83). San Francisco: Jossey-Bass.

HARGENS, L. L., RASKIN, B. F., and ALLISON, P. D. (1976) "Problems in estimating measurement error from panel data: An example involving the measurement of scientific productivity." *Sociological Methods & Research* 4: 439-458.

HAYDUK, L. A. (1987) *Structural Equation Modeling With LISREL: Essentials and Advances*. Baltimore: Johns Hopkins University Press.

HEISE, D. R. (1969) "Separating reliability and stability in test-retest correlation." *American Sociological Review* 34: 93-101.

HENDRICKSON, L., and JONES, B. (1987) "A study of longitudinal causal models comparing gain score analysis with structural equation approaches." In P. Cuttance and R. Ecob (Eds.), *Structural Modeling by Example* (pp. 86-107). Cambridge: Cambridge University Press.

JAGODZINSKI, W., KÜHNEL, S. M., and SCHMIDT, P. (1987) "Is there a 'socratic effect' in nonexperimental panel studies?" *Sociological Methods & Research* 15: 259-302.

JENNINGS, M. K., and NIEMI, R. (1975) "Continuity and change in political orientations: A longitudinal study of two generations." *American Political Science Review* 69: 1316-1355.

JOHNSTON, J. (1972) *Econometric Methods*. New York: McGraw-Hill.

JÖRESKOG, K. G., and SÖRBOM, D. (1976) "Statistical models and methods for analysis of longitudinal data." In D. J. Aigner and A. S. Goldberger (Eds.), *Latent Variables in Socioeconomic Models* (pp. 285-325). Amsterdam: North Holland.

JÖRESKOG, K. G., and SÖRBOM, D. (1989) *LISREL 7: A guide to the Program and Applications*. Chicago: SPSS.

JUDD, C. M., and KENNY, D. A. (1981) *Estimating the Effects of Social Interventions*. Cambridge: Cambridge University Press.

JUDD, C. M., KROSNICK, J., and MILBURN, M. A. (1981) "Political involvement and attitude structure in the general public." *American Sociological Review* 46: 660-669.

KENNY, D. A. (1973) "Cross-lagged and synchronous common factors in panel data." In A. S. Goldberger and O. D. Duncan (Eds.), *Structural Equation Models in the Social Sciences* (pp. 153-165). New York: Seminar Press.

KESSLER, R. C., and GREENBERG, D. F. (1981) *Linear Panel Analysis*. New York: Academic Press.

LIKER, J. K., AUGUSTYNIAK, S., and DUNCAN, G. J. (1985) "Panel data and models of change: A comparison of first difference and conventional two-wave models." *Social Science Research* 14: 80-101.

LONG, J. S. (1983a) *Confirmatory Factor Analysis.* Sage University Paper series on Quantitative Applications in the Social Sciences, 07-033. Beverly Hills, CA: Sage.

LONG, J. S. (1983b) *Covariance Structure Models: An Introduction to LISREL.* Sage University Paper series on Quantitative Applications in the Social Sciences, 07-034. Beverly Hills, CA: Sage.

MARKUS, G. B. (1979) *Analyzing Panel Data.* Sage University Paper series on Quantitative Applications in the Social Sciences, 07-018. Beverly Hills, CA: Sage.

MARKUS, G. B. (1982) "Political attitudes in an election year." *American Political Science Review* 76: 538-560.

MAYER, L. S., and CARROLL, S. S. (1987) "Testing for lagged, cotemporal and total dependence in cross-lagged panel analysis." *Sociological Methods & Research* 16: 187-217.

McADAMS, J. (1986) "Alternatives for dealing with errors in the variables: An example using panel data." *American Journal of Political Science* 30: 256-278.

McARDLE, J. J., and ABER, M. S. (1990) "Patterns of change within latent variable structural equation models." In A. Von Eye (Ed.), *Statistical Methods in Longitudinal Research, Volume 1: Principles and Structuring Change* (pp. 151-24). San Diego: Academic Press.

McDONALD, R. P. (1980) "A simple comprehensive model for the analysis of covariance structures: Some remarks on application." *British Journal of Mathematical and Statistical Psychology* 33: 161-183.

MENARD, S. (1991) *Longitudinal Research.* Sage University Paper series on Quantitative Applications in the Social Sciences, 07-076. Newbury Park, CA: Sage.

MENARD, S., and ELLIOTT, D. S. (1990) "Longitudinal and cross-sectional data collection and analysis in the study of crime and delinquency." *Justice Quarterly* 7: 11-55.

NESSELROADE, J. R., STIGLER, S. M., and BALTES, P. B. (1980) "Regression toward the mean and the study of change." *Psychological Bulletin* 88: 622-637.

OSTROM, C. W. (1978) *Time Series Analysis: Regression Techniques.* Sage University Paper series on Quantitative Applications in the Social Sciences, 07-009. Beverly Hills, CA: Sage.

PALMQUIST, B., and GREEN, D. (1989, September) "Estimation of correlated measurement errors in panel data." Paper presented at the annual meeting of the American Political Science Association, Washington, DC.

PLEWIS, I. (1985) *Analysing Change: Measurement and Exploration Using Longitudinal Data.* Chichester, UK: John Wiley.

PORST, R., SCHMIDT, P., and ZEIFANG, K. (1987) "Comparison of subgroups by models with multiple indicators." *Sociological Methods & Research* 15: 303-315.

RAFFOLOVICH, L. E., and BOHRNSTEDT, G. W. (1987) "Common, specific and error variance components of factor models: Estimation with longitudinal data." *Sociological Methods & Research* 15: 385-405.

RINDSKOPF, D. M. (1984) "Using phantom and imaginary latent variables to parametrize constraints in linear structural models." *Psychometrika* 49: 37-47.

ROGOSA, D. (1979) "Causal models in longitudinal research: Rationale, formulation, and interpretation." In J. R. Nesselroade and P. B. Baltes (Eds.), *Longitudinal Research in the Study of Behavior and Development* (pp. 263-302). New York: Academic Press.

SAYRS, L. W. (1989) *Pooled Time Series Analysis.* Sage University Paper series on Quantitative Applications in the Social Sciences, 07-070. Newbury Park, CA: Sage.

SHINGLES, R. D. (1976) "Causal inference in cross-lagged panel analysis." *Political Methodology* 3: 95-133.

STIMSON, J. A. (1985) "Regression in space and time: A statistical essay." *American Journal of Political Science* 29: 914-947.

SULLIVAN, J., and FELDMAN, S. (1979) *Multiple Indicators: An Introduction.* Sage University Paper series on Quantitative Applications in the Social Sciences, 07-015. Beverly Hills, CA: Sage.

TUMA, N., and HANNAN, M. (1984) *Social Dynamics.* New York: Academic Press.

WERTS, C. E., JÖRESKOG, K. G., and LINN, R. L. (1971) "Comment on 'The estimation of measurement error in panel data'." *American Sociological Review* 36: 110-113.

WHEATON, B., MUTHEN, B., ALWIN, D. F., and SUMMERS, G. F. (1977) "Assessing reliability and stability in panel models." In D. R. Heise (Ed.), *Sociological Methodology 1977* (pp. 84-136). San Francisco: Jossey-Bass.

WILEY, D. E., and WILEY, J. A. (1970) "The estimation of measurement error in panel data." *American Sociological Review* 35: 112-117.

WILEY, J. A., and WILEY, M. G. (1974) "A note on correlated errors in repeated measurements." *Sociological Methods & Research* 3: 172-88.

ABOUT THE AUTHOR

STEVEN E. FINKEL is Associate Professor of Government and Foreign Affairs at the University of Virginia. He received his Ph.D. in Political Science in 1984 from the State University of New York at Stony Brook. Dr. Finkel has published articles on political participation and public opinion, his primary substantive areas of interest, and on quantitative methods in scholarly journals such as *American Political Science Review*, *American Journal of Political Science*, *Journal of Politics*, and *Public Opinion Quarterly*.